THE SIEGE WITHIN

LONDON BOROUGH OF ENFIELD

PONDERS END LIBRARY
COLLEGE COURT, ENFIELD EN3 4EY

No. H 22425

This book to be RETURNED on or before the latest date stamped below unless a renewal has been obtained by personal call, post or telephone, quoting the above number and the date due for return.

-4. FEB. 1978
-1 JUL 1978
26 SEP 1978
-5 DEC 1978
19 SEP 1979
-5. SEP. 1980

In the case of infectious illness, do not return books to the Library, but inform the Librarian.

By the same author:

THE ONE REMAINS
THE LIFE AND TIMES OF HEROD THE GREAT
THE LATER HERODS
HADRIAN
CAESARS AND SAINTS
JERUSALEM (J. M. Dent and Sons)
THE END OF THE ROMAN WORLD
DEATH OF THE ROMAN REPUBLIC
ROMAN MYTHOLOGY (Hamlyn)

In paperback

THE POLITICAL BACKGROUND OF THE NEW TESTAMENT (*The Later Herods*)

THE PILGRIM'S COMPANIONS

In Jerusalem and Bethlehem
In Athens
In Rome

THE SIEGE WITHIN THE WALLS

MALTA 1940–1943

by

STEWART PEROWNE

HODDER AND STOUGHTON

Copyright © 1970 *by Stewart Perowne*

First printed 1970

SBN 340 02954 4

All rights reserved. No part of this publication may be reproduced or transmitted in any form or by any means, electronic or mechanical, including photocopy, recording, or any information storage and retrieval system, without permission in writing from the publisher.

Printed in Great Britain for Hodder and Stoughton Limited, St Paul's House, Warwick Lane, London, E.C.4 by Ebenezer Baylis and Son, Limited, The Trinity Press, Worcester, and London

To

MABEL–

inevitably

"It was a damned nice thing, the nearest run thing you ever saw in your life."

The Duke of Wellington, on the battle of Waterloo

ACKNOWLEDGEMENTS

The author is grateful to the following for permission to use material from their publications:

Messrs William Collins, Sons and Co, Ltd for extracts from *The Turn of the Tide*: War Diaries of Field Marshal Lord Alanbrooke (ed. Arthur Bryant); A. P. Watt and Son, Messrs Hutchison and Co, Ltd, and the Estate of Viscount Cunningham of Hyndhope for extracts from *A Sailor's Odyssey* by Admiral of the Fleet, Viscount Cunningham of Hyndhope; Messrs Cassell and Company Ltd for extracts from *The Second World War*, Volumes I, II, III, IV by Sir Winston Churchill; Messrs B. T. Batsford Ltd for extracts from *The Battle for the Mediterranean* by Donald Macintyre; Ufficio Storico della Marina Militare for extracts from *Operazione C3: Malta*; Sir Arturo Mercieca for extracts from his autobiography *Le Mie Viecende.*

The author is also grateful to Air Chief Marshal Sir Keith Park, Miss Mabel Strickland and Mr Macdonald Hastings for permission to quote from their radio broadcasts, and to Mrs Audrey Boyd for permission to quote from the broadcast made by her late husband, Admiral Sir Denis Boyd.

The author also wishes to thank Mrs Queenie Lee and Mrs Norman whom he has unfortunately been unable to contact to request permission to use their extracts.

CONTENTS

ILLUSTRATIONS

Key to Acknowledgements

1 Imperial War Museum
2 Ufficio Storico della Marina Militare, Rome
3 *Times of Malta*
4 Graham Binns
5 John Dei Conti Manduca

PROLOGUE

No epoch is ever so remote from us as that which we have just left. Thousands of us can recall with precise clarity the events of the 15th March, 44 B.C., when Julius Caesar was struck down in the portico of Pompey in Rome, but would find it hard to recount with accuracy what happened in Cuba in 1964. There is, as Thomas Hardy pointed out, a limbo to which events are consigned when they have ceased to be news and have not yet become history. Many aspects of the hideous prism of the war of 1939–45 are still, for that reason, obscure. A flash here, an optical illusion there, but no steady light.

Malta has been like that. During the war and immediately after it a number of books were written about Malta. The best of them were good journalism, but constrained still by the trammels of 'security'. The worst of them were English sentiment at its most emetic. More recently, books have appeared such as *Malta Convoy* and *The Battle for the Mediterranean* which give objective and well-informed accounts of the events they set out to record. Both are very good books. So far, no similar attempt has been made to tell the tale from within Malta itself, that is, the story of Malta at war from the Maltese point of view. Nor can the present study do more than perhaps provide some indicators for a future historian. As suggested above it is still too early for that. *Temps perdu*, time lost, those days before yesterday, how justly Proust described them.

Many of those who took part in Malta's battles of twenty-five years ago are dead. The survivors are curiously reticent. Not that they are not willing to furnish any scrap of information which may be of use to a recorder. On the contrary they will do all in their power to help him. But there is a psychological obstacle to be overcome. The time really is 'lost', and it is a hard task to recover it. I feel that myself. After visiting a friend, and going over with him memories of the war, documents perhaps relating to his war duties, I come out into the bright sunlight of Malta at peace, hear the children at play, look down into the Grand Harbour from which Italian and German tourists are coming up to admire and to purchase—I find it hard to realise that five minutes ago I was listening to tales of death and destruction, of ruin and survival in this same square, where the flowers grow and the transistors howl.

The very fabric of Malta gives you this same double focus. Only those who knew Valetta before the war would know that the Palace had been bombed, that the tranquil Ionic portico of the Courts of Justice stands on the site of a predecessor which was blown to smithereens, or that the fabric of the Casino Maltese, one of the most delightful clubs in Europe, was reduced to rubble and is only half what it externally appears to be, the Treasury of the Knights. Even the ruins of Barry's Opera House have taken on a sort of Piranesi air, which clothes them in the picturesque rather than the pathetic.

It is down in the Ditch, the gigantic fosse which separates Valetta from Floriana on the north, that this doubleness, I had almost said duplicity, of history is most assertive. The fosse is crossed by three viaducts. One once carried the Valetta-Medina railway, a second bears Nelson avenue, which links the city with the Harbour, the third, biggest and newest, forms the main entry into the capital. Both these latter roadways are abuzz with movement. You can see the folk scurrying along them, hear the traffic, experience the whole kaleidoscope of contemporary, busy Malta. If you look upwards that is: the ditch is a hundred feet deep. At eye-level you are looking at Malta at war. There is little sound, down here. No traffic. Only the rock on either side, the great, pitted walls rising to the blue sky. In the walls are numbers of little doorways, with numbers stencilled on their blocked entrances *CD 29*, and so on. They are the property of the Civil Defence Department. One, for some reason, is not blocked up, but accessible by means of a rusty iron door, swinging on its creaking hinges. Above it there is another, unofficial, number still just decipherable, *73*. And hard by a neat plaque, inscribed *K.O.M.R. 1940*. The recess, for it is no more, behind the door is rank and dark, low, cramped, like some prehistoric tomb. It was no tomb, it was a home, the home of a family whose dwelling had been destroyed, and who had found a refuge here, in this cave which they had hewn with their own hands, and to which they had given the street number of their former house. The King's Own Malta Regiment had a post hard by. Down here, in the silent fosse Malta really is at war. It makes you feel like Tennyson standing on the bridge at Coventry, and makes you want to try to put together some at least of the tesserae of the vanished, dispersed mosaic. The following pages are an attempt to do so.

As you try to pick up the bits, to re-form the design, you are reminded of Seneca's finest play. Medea is at bay, and her old nurse is trying to persuade her to give in. "What's the good of going on?" she says "Your friends have deserted you, your own countrymen are far away, your resources are spent. *Quid jam superest?*" "What remains?" "*Medea superest!*" is the great answer. "Medea remains." The same question was put to Malta in 1942. She gave the same answer: "*Melita superest.*"

Mdina, Eve of All Saints, 1968.

ACT ONE

I

THE SEAT OF DAMOCLES

1939

On the 22nd August, 1939, I was having dinner with Lord and Lady Astor in St James's, Geoffrey Dawson, then editor of *The Times*, being the other guest. "We know now there's going to be a war," said Waldorf Astor, most pacific of men, "What do you think we need to win it?" I was taken aback by this question. Nancy Astor started to answer, but Waldorf said, "No, I want to hear what Stewart thinks." "Well," I said, "I can only speak for the small part of the world I know, that is the Mediterranean. There, we need three things, an alliance with Russia, an understanding with Turkey and Mr Churchill."

At that time we had none of them; and it was in this mood of blank foreboding that I joined the miscellaneous rabble at Victoria next evening, composed of those of us—some hundreds—who had been ordered to entrain there to join a convoy which would take us back to our posts. There were diplomatists, Cable and Wireless staff, soldiers and Colonial officers. Organised chaos reigned, and my spirits fell ever lower: could we win a war if we couldn't even arrange a railway journey? The same mood prevailed all that night as we crossed the Channel, and during the following day as we slowly and haltingly steamed across France. Only when we reached Marseilles did confidence revive; for there was H.M.S. *Shropshire*, waiting for us to embark, and there at the head of the gangway was my old friend Father (now Monsignor) Cyril Damian Fay. All at once assurance ousted mistrust. With the Navy about, all would be well. It was. Somehow the *Shropshire* absorbed us all, and fed us, and bedded us, and carried us on our way.

When we put into Malta, I asked for special permission to disembark for an hour or two, with two friends, the late Sir Robin Furness and the late Sir Walter Smart, both of whom were returning to Cairo. On landing I made a telephone call, and then we motored up to the old capital, Mdina, and rang the bell of the Casa Inguanez.

This palace has been the home of the Inguanez family for centuries. Malta has its own nobility, some thirty titles of which have been recognised by the English Crown ever since the Island became associated with Great Britain. Most of them are eighteenth century creations of successive Grand Masters; but the Inguanez barony goes back to the days when the Kings of Aragon ruled Malta. Maltese titles can descend in various ways; some only to males (though they may pass through females), others to members of either sex. The Inguanez title, the oldest in the land, is one of the latter; and so it came about that the present holder was Mary Scibberras D'Amico Trigona Inguanez, one of the most beautiful and witty women of her age. The Maltese nobility is entitled to send two representatives to the coronation of English sovereigns. Mary Inguanez had been one such on three occasions. She was the friend of many members of the Royal Family, and always carried herself royally: whether in her own drawing-room or on a rock at a seaside picnic she was equally at her ease. She always sat upright, like a flower, never leaning against the back of a chair (if there was one), and her hands, expressive as Duse's, when not employed to make some telling point, remained in her lap. She had been married to a Scottish colonel, but was now a widow.

The Baroness was awaiting us, in the room which bears an inscription on the wall to the effect that in this room where her ancestor has entertained King Alfonso I, the Baroness had entertained his descendant King Alfonso XIII. On the table stood a decanter and four glasses. "The Waterloo Madeira," said the Baroness, with that slightly bi-focal roguish smile of hers. "Oh, but how good of you . . ." "Well, I'd rather you and your distinguished friends had it than THEY did—NO! I don't mean the Italians, I mean my relations!"

This episode may seem to be egotistically irrelevant, but I have recalled it for a double reason. First, because it may show how instinctively an Englishman, however downcast by the blunders of bureaucrats, and the folly of rulers, rallies on contact with the Royal Navy. "The Navy is in every Englishman's bones", as Admiral Sir William Fisher, 'The Great Agrippa', once remarked without a trace of self-consciousness. For more than a century the Maltese people had been intimately associated with the Royal Navy. Thousands of them had served in Her and His Majesty's ships, thousands have manned the Malta dockyard. Thus generation after generation of Maltese had come to share the Englishman's feeling for the Navy, his absolute trust in it, in a way that no other nation on earth had done. This was to have a vital influence on the spirit of Malta during the war, and hence on her survival. Secondly, at Casa Inguanez we had been conscious of two things. The first was the age-long unbroken tradition of this noble family. It is of Aragonese origin. It had survived the Knights, it had survived the French: it would survive the Fascists. War was at hand, yes, the Baroness knew that as well as anyone; but she awaited it with almost a 'frolic welcome'. So did many more of her fellow-citizens.

War did not actually break out until a week later; but for Malta it had in a sense begun three years before.

Even before his Abyssinian adventure, Mussolini had had his eyes on Malta –*Malta nostra* as he called it. He neglected no method, fair or foul, but mostly foul, to create a 'fifth column' in the Island. 'Cultural' ties, the press, consuls, tarts, even the Church, by a shocking exploitation of the 1929 concordat with the Vatican, was abused as an agent of *Italianità*. No horse is so dead today as the war-horse of yesterday, and there is no point in flogging it; yet something must be said of the dreary, hoary 'Language Question', because it was in its day (like Women's Suffrage or Home Rule) a burning cause of strife.

In the words of Mr J. Aquilina, Professor of Maltese in the Royal Malta University, "The Maltese speak a language, the grammar and syntax of which are predominantly Arabic, with a vocabulary partly Arabic and partly old Sicilian and Italian with a number of more recent loanwords. The language goes back to 870 when the Arabs conquered the Maltese Islands . . ." (*The Times*, 26th October, 1968).

The reason the language caught on is that the Maltese are ethnically Semitic, and that before the advent of the Arabs they already spoke a Semitic, that is, Punic tongue.

To cite Professor Aquilina again: "The language is about the only relic of Arab domination left in Malta. Because they have always been Christian and culturally tied to Sicily and Italy, for several centuries the Maltese intelligentsia used Italian for their literary self-expression and official correspondence, including legal and notarial documents.

"For many years before the Second World War, not only Maltese but also English were opposed by the intelligentsia especially the clergy and the legal class, who resisted any attempt to reduce the official status of Italian."

The issue was complicated further by the fact that although Maltese had been spoken for more than a millennium, it had never until quite recently become a written language (if we except a poem here and there—a folk-ballad or two). It was only natural therefore that the language of the neighbouring peninsula should be adopted. The Knights, it is true, spoke French; but the Knights kept themselves very much to themselves, as is the manner of expatriates. When the French occupied Malta under Bonaparte, however, they made French the official language, and started giving the streets French names. (Hitherto they had had no names: as in other ancient cities, the districts were known simply as 'the quarter of the jewellers', 'the ascent of the goldsmiths' and so on). Two years later, when the English arrived, they did away with the French names and substituted, not English, but Italian ones. Strada Reale, or Kingsway as it is now called, was so named in honour of King George III. They went further: the English made Italian the language of the law-courts. How they did so, and after what prolonged wrangles and discussions, has recently been lucidly shown by Dr Hugh Harding, a Maltese jurisprudent and son of a distinguished Maltese judge, in his book *English Legislation in Malta*.

It was thus hard for the English to eradicate a usage they had themselves introduced. In the end they did so, not by replacing Italian by English, but by elevating Maltese. Italian lost its official status in 1934. Article 5 of the Constitution of Independent Malta makes Maltese the national language.

Such in outline is the history of this once burning question, now cold as clinker. In 1936, it was a cause of acute division, subtly exploited by the Fascists. To add to this internal unease, there was added the real and imminent danger of invasion. When sanctions were half-heartedly imposed on Italy by the League of Nations, it was known that if they were tightened up to the point of denying him oil, Mussolini would declare war. And his first target would be Malta.

At once the Island was put upon a war footing. The first sign of the new situation was depressing. The whole fleet, the largest, most powerful ever assembled by any nation, disappeared. The Grand Harbour, which sheltered two squadrons of battleships, a cruiser squadron, an aircraft-carrier and a battle-cruiser, became a deserted pool. On the other side of Valetta, two flotillas of destroyers and two of submarines left Marsamxett: it, too, became a forlorn lake. The whole fleet had sailed away to Alexandria.

In Malta itself, civil defence was organised. The populace were urged to apply for gas-masks. The government set about preparing refuges against gas-attack, for such it was deemed would be the form the onslaught would take. This meant that in the height of the summer's heat, rooms had to be found which could be made even more humid and stifling by sealing every possible vent against the intrusion of the deadly fumes. The old passages, hewn in the rock beneath the main streets of Valetta by the Knights, were re-explored; and it was found that in emergency it was possible to walk from the Palace to the military headquarters in the Auberge de Castile underground all the way.

At that time 'the government' meant a small but highly qualified team, directed by the Lieutenant-Governor, Sir Harry Luke, since the constitution was in one of its periodical phases of suspension. The Treasurer was Major Galizia, the Secretary to Government,

Mr Edward Mifsud, the Attorney-General, Sir Philip Pullicino, the Director of Medical Services, Professor Bernard, the Director of Public Works, Professor John Gatt, the Director of Education, Dr Albert Laferla, the Commissioner of Police, Mr Salvo Galea. They worked together in the most effective harmony.

The most significant exercise, in view of the years to come, was a night air reconnaissance, to ascertain how visible Malta was from the sky. At that time, the government possessed no legal power to compel people to show no lights. An appeal was therefore made, over the Rediffusion system and in the press, that on such and such a night no lights whatever should be shown between certain hours. The result was amazing. A detachment of flying-boats took to the air, and after cruising some miles away from Malta, turned and came back over the two Islands. Their presence was eventually signalled by the bright ring of surf around the shores, a silver chain, as it were, to fix the location of the target. Within the chain, there was absolute darkness. With two exceptions, not a light was to be seen anywhere, neither in Malta nor in Gozo, neither in the towns nor in the remote farms. The two exceptions were the valves of the admiralty wireless station near Fort Ricasoli: it was essential that the station should be in continuous operation, and in those days that meant the employment of large and luminous valves, which must be cooled by a constant flow of fresh air. The other exception was a certain colonel who had got tired, and had decided to motor home.

This unanimity was remarkable, and a wonderful proof of the solidarity of the Maltese people with their British protectors. Despite all that Mussolini had done, it was now clear that the bulk of the people would have nothing to do with him, that they would stand foursquare with England.

This exercise had one curious by-product. It was described in the London *Times* as 'a trial occultation of lights', which it was. But it gave birth to the term 'blackout' as generally used. The reason was that nearly all those concerned in its organisation were members of the Malta Amateur Dramatic Club, and therefore naturally used the theatrical term for the sudden darkening of a stage, which had been imported from America some years before, and was now in regular use by the Club. As thus established on that night in Malta, 'black-out' became a current technical term.

A cardinal factor in the solidarity of Maltese and English was the calibre and outlook of the Englishmen at the head of affairs. There were three. The Governor was Sir Charles Bonham-Carter, one of that remarkable brood of brothers who adorned their generation in so many different fields. Sir Charles was a man of wide culture and winning manners. Lady Bonham-Carter was an artist of great charm. Both husband and wife set out from the beginning of his term of office in 1937 to get to know the Maltese people, in every walk of life. They would visit the villages, and meet the citizens in the clubs—for in every Maltese town and village there are one or more band clubs, a typical Maltese social institution, often productive of both harmony and discord. Lady Bonham-Carter made the welfare of hospital patients and the old and infirm her particular concern. The Maltese, always quick to return affection, took the Bonham-Carters to their hearts.

The second member of the triad was Admiral Fisher already mentioned. William Wordsworth Fisher was a great man. "William is mighty," Lady Fisher used to say. Tall, majestic of aspect, with just the touch of theatricality that goes with majesty—the profane said he sat on a soap-box, as he swept along in his canary-yellow open Rolls-Royce. A fine sailor and a fine commander. He, too, was a man of the lettered world, brother of H. A. L. Fisher the historian and cabinet minister. Lady Fisher had been bred into the world of literature, her father having been Dr Warre-Cornish the vice-provost of Eton. Admiralty House during the Fisher régime was a miniature court, whither flowed all that was talented and interesting. The Fishers had known and loved Malta and the Maltese from the days when 'WW' was a junior officer. Them too the Maltese justly regarded as personal friends.

To give but one example of Sir William's solicitude for his Maltese friends. Normally in peace time, numbers of watermen made a good living by conveying officers, ratings and visitors to and from His Majesty's ships in both harbours. With the Fleet gone, as it was during the Abyssinian crisis, the watermen suffered great privation. They were not forgotten. Amid all his cares, Admiral Fisher thought of them. He came back to Malta on a flying visit, during which he summoned me to Admiralty House. "How many dghaisa-men (for as such the watermen are known) are there in Malta?" "I don't know, sir, but I will let you know tomorrow morning." I did—it was several hundred. The Commander-in-Chief returned to Alexandria, sent a 'brief' round the fleet, which resulted in each waterman receiving a little present. The amount was not much, but the effect on their feelings, the knowledge that they were remembered by their absent friends, may be imagined.

The third triumvir was Sir Harry Luke, the Lieutenant-Governor. In those days of military Governors of Malta, if fell to the Lieutenant-Governor to oversee the civil, or internal, government of the Island, the Governor being primarily concerned with Service affairs. At the time of the Abyssinian crisis, owing to political discord within the Island fomented by agents from without, the constitution was in suspense, and the Island was ruled by a small conciliar body, which came to be known as 'The Palace Clique'. This meant in effect, Sir Harry Luke and three very able Maltese colleagues. Sir Harry, the fine flower of Eton and Oxford, had nevertheless had the advantage of a cosmopolitan upbringing. From an early age he was intimately acquainted with most European countries, and with their politics. He was an adept at all things ecclesiastical. He was a polished linguist. As a young man he served in the district administration of Cyprus, where he added Greek and Turkish to his more conventional languages. During the first war, he had served on the staff of the Commander-in-Chief of the allied naval forces in the Aegean, and had then become High Commissioner in the Caucasus. Before coming to Malta in 1930, he had served with great distinction and courage in Palestine. In short Sir Harry was the ideal choice for Lieutenant-Governor in those troubled years. There was no quirk in the political labyrinth he did not know, no ecclesiastical gambit which he could not forestall. Before him Fascist intrigue was powerless, because Sir Harry always got in first. He too, from the very beginning of his long and beneficent tenure of office in Malta, showed himself the friend of the Maltese nation, not only of contemporary

Malta for which he did so much, but of their artistic and cultural heritage. So many of the monuments which now attract tourists to Malta, even the mediaeval window which adorns one of the stamps, owe their preservation to Sir Harry Luke.

When war broke out the only one of the big three remaining in Malta was the Governor, the other two having been transferred to other spheres; but their work remained. The foundations were secure, Malta would not waver.

Finally, in this brief survey of morale, must be mentioned the most important factor of all, religious faith. The Maltese are a truly, deeply religious people. They are devout Roman Catholic Christians. On all hands you see the outward signs of it. At almost every street-corner some saint stands on point duty with upraised hand, by nearly every door there is a little shrine. Every home has its sacred symbol illuminated in a place of honour. The church is the centre of the life of town and village alike, and the priests are the honoured and trusted counsellors of their flocks. The discipline of being not only subjects of the British crown but citizens of a kingdom not of this world sustained the Maltese nation when the kingdoms of this world collapsed.

2

ENIGMA VARIATIONS

1939–40

Before attempting to plot the progress of the war as it affected Malta, and equally as Malta affected it, it will be necessary to make one or two general observations, if the story is not to be either banal, or so complex as to be unintelligible. First, the idea that once the war broke out, Malta was simply (as someone thoughtlessly dubbed it) 'an unsinkable aircraft-carrier', that all Malta had to do was to be a 'tight little island' a sort of geographical hedgehog, is rubbish. Malta was extremely vulnerable. For a century and a half Malta, a British island in an Italo-Arab sea, had been a political anomaly. With the advent of war, it became a strategic paradox, an offensive outpost which was a major defensive liability.

Secondly, far from being a single action, with a beginning, a middle and an end, the siege of Malta was more like the action of a clock, the pendulum oscillating all the time, checks and balances rising and falling continuously; for Malta did not depend on herself, strategically or logistically, but was always at the mercy of campaigns in other lands, Greece, Crete, Egypt, Cyrenaica, Tunisia and finally Sicily and Italy, and on the naval and air encounters that those campaigns entailed. Thus no-one in Malta could possibly tell from week to week what the future held for the Island. It was on these ever-shifting shoals that its defenders had to try to build some sort of breastwork. Thirdly, when it comes to strategy, a layman, looking back on the planning of both sides is struck by their curiously ambivalent attitude to their armaments. So often it seems that they had no precise idea of what either they or their opponents could or could not do. For instance, what was to be the rôle of the battleship?

Writing of the battle of Taranto, which took place on the night of the 11/12th November, 1940, that is only five months after Mussolini had dragged his country into the war, Donald Macintyre in his excellent *The Battle for the Mediterranean* has this to say:

"The scene which greeted the eye in Taranto harbour at dawn on the 12th November, marked, for those who had eyes to see, the end of the battleship era", because the victory had been gained solely by the skill and daring of forty-two aviators, armed with torpedoes, launched into the air from the deck of the carrier *Illustrious*. To quote Macintyre again: "The relative strength of the two battle-fleets had now been reversed in favour of the British. Only two battleships remained available to the Italians against five in Cunningham's fleet. In his autobiography Andrew Cunningham has said that 'The crippling of half the Italian battle-fleet at a blow at Taranto had a profound effect on the naval strategical situation in the Mediterranean'. This judgement is open to doubt" since "basically the naval situation in the Mediterranean remained virtually unchanged because battleships were no longer the linch-pin of power. Each side lacked in some degree the element upon which control of the sea had come to depend—naval air strength, offensive and defensive."

The situation could not be better put—'for those who had eyes to see'. But how many had? And if after Taranto, why not before? Why not at the outbreak of war with Italy, when the entire fleet had to repair to Egypt? Or for that matter, why not during the Abyssinian crisis three years earlier, when the same manœuvre had been found expedient? And yet in the very next year, the appalling disaster involved in the loss by Japanese air attack of the *Prince of Wales* and the *Repulse* was caused simply because certain eyes which should have seen had not, even then, done so.

When we survey air strategy, the same ambivalence is to be found. What is the prime air objective? Is it to protect, to 'neutralise' by pulverisation, or to occupy? As to the desirability and practicability of the first, all the warring air forces were agreed: you had to shoot down your enemy before he shot you down or preferably shoot him sitting. But when it comes to neutralisation, there was just as much wishful bombing in those days as there has been in Vietnam in a later era. I can myself remember that when I first went to Aden as a Political Officer in 1937, I was told that the Protectorate was kept in order by Air Control, and that the employment of 'ground personnel' was out of the question; but it was soon found that ground personnel were essential to effective and continuing control, and a corps of Government Guards was enlisted. We shall come upon 'neutralisation' in the story of Malta. And we shall meet occupation, too, both attempted and unattempted. And we shall see that what looked like the most brilliant example of occupation, namely the capture of Crete by the *Luftwaffe*, led to its own undoing and so to the salvation of Malta and the Allied victory in the Mediterranean.

To make matters more complicated, there was not merely a lack of unanimity in the direction of British war policy in regard to Malta, there was acute disagreement. Of this dangerous flaw, Oliver Warner, in his *Cunningham of Hyndhope, Admiral of the Fleet* gives a concise description: As early as 1938 "The Air Ministry view was that in time of war, with Italian airfields a bare sixty miles away in Sicily, it was improbable that the Island could be defended. The War office were inclined to agree and no argument that Backhouse brought forward would change them." (Admiral Backhouse was at that time First Sea Lord.)

Fortunately for Malta and the allied cause others held the opposite view. One, as will later be seen, was Churchill himself. Another was the Commander-in-Chief, Mediterranean, Admiral Cunningham. During the crisis of 1942, Cunningham wrote to a brother officer from London, whither he had been summoned by the Prime Minister, "My heart remains in the Mediterranean. I was told the other day that Nelson once said: 'Waking or sleeping Malta is always in my thoughts', and that exactly describes my case."

In Malta itself, where the memory of the Abyssinian war and its attendant risks to the Island were still fresh in men's minds, every feasible step was taken to prepare the populace for a possible war. District Councils were organised for the purpose of recruiting Air Raid Wardens. These councils included as a rule the Parish Priest, the District Medical Officer, the Head Teacher, and representatives of the local band clubs and one or two notables. Their duties were prescribed precisely, as follows:

In Peace Time.

1. To recruit an adequate number of Air Raid Wardens for their respective Districts.
2. When Air Raid Wardens have passed their course of lectures and are definitely enrolled, to allot them to sectors or streets in their Districts.
3. To see that Air Raid Wardens perform the duties entrusted to them, the most important of which is to keep in close touch with the people in their sector, to advise them on the precautions they should take and generally to keep them in a state of preparedness for any emergency.
4. To report to the Central Committee any case where replacement of individual Air Raid Wardens becomes necessary and to take steps for recruiting substitutes.
5. To submit to the Central Committee any suggestions they may think fit to make to ensure greater efficiency in their Districts.
6. To maintain regular contact with the Central Committee by seeing that their delegates attend the monthly meetings to submit reports which have been approved by their Councils.

In War Time.

In addition to (4), (5) and (6) above.

1. To supervise the work of Air Raid Wardens in their Districts.
2. To help the Evacuation and Billeting Staffs as requested and in so far as it may lie in their power to do so.
3. As a branch of the Food Control Board, to carry out the orders issued to them by the Food Control Board.

14th July, 1939.

As regards the geological structure and populace of the Island, two points must be made. The Island consists physically almost wholly of rock, the same rock as supplied the material for the gigantic structures of the Neolithic Age, which still after five thousand years command our bewildered admiration, and has furnished the building material of Malta ever since, down to our own day. Only in the very grandest structures has wood ever been used even for beams, because it had to be brought, generally towed behind ships in order to season it, from Sicily; which means that the towns and villages of Malta offer a fire-risk smaller than any other country in the world. This was a saving boon to Malta during the war. This same rock is very easily mined and quarried; that too helped to save Malta, because nowhere else was it so easy to excavate bomb-proof shelters. Thousands found in them a sure refuge.

The second point is that although Malta is very thickly populated, the population is very unevenly distributed. Around the harbours (by and on which the majority of the population have lived for so long) it is dense; but in the northern area it is so thin that even today it is possible to motor from Mdina to Marfa, the port for Gozo, a distance of nearly eight miles, without passing through a single village. To quote the latest census figures (November 1967), and the proportion of rural to urban had changed but little in twenty-five years: "Malta's urban population is concentrated in the towns round Grand Harbour and Marsamxett Harbour, which flank Valetta on both sides. The inner Harbour region which consisted of parishes having some frontage on these two harbours, housed 39.8% of the total urban population, which at 296,360 made up 94.3% of the 314,216 persons enumerated at the census." The outer Harbour region accounted for another 23.8% of the urban population, the remainder being housed in towns such as Mdina-Rabat and the larger *casals*, as Maltese built-up areas, half village, half town, are more euphoniously styled. Even in 1967, according to the census, the total built-up area amounted to only 14·529 square miles out of an overall land area of 121.350 square miles. Allowing for the uncultivatable tract, this still leaves a large proportion of the area of Malta free for agriculture, again another vital factor in its war life.

The actual outbreak of war seems to have made little impact on Malta. The Island was used to war-scares. First there had been the Abyssinian crisis. Nothing happened. Then at Easter 1939 came the Italian invasion of Albania. Again nothing happened. I will quote from two who were in Malta at the time. First the then Chief Justice, Sir Arturo Mercieca, who was ardently and eloquently pro-

Italian. In his autobiography (the original is in Italian) he writes: "England and France after having ineffectively requested the Führer to withdraw his troops (from Poland), declared that they were in a state of war with Germany as from the 3rd September. Mussolini, after holding a Council of Ministers, let it be known that he had taken no initiative of a military character. This in some measure calmed the tension which had arisen in Malta, already accentuated by the general mobilisation, by the promulgation 'rat-a-tat-tat' (*a tamburro battente*) of various emergency legislation, and by the distribution of gas-masks to the entire population. Everyone prepared for a war of brief duration, given the vast quantities of lethal weapons collected by the belligerents. Received therefore with scepticism was the prediction made in England by the War Council that a war lasting at least three years was to be expected."

"There was something rather sinister about the first eight months of the war", writes Mrs Norman in her charming book *For Gallantry*. "We expected so much to happen and had nerved ourselves for the crash and nothing happened. It must have been the same everywhere in Europe.

"It was a mercy for Malta that we had that respite for it gave the Island a little more time to put her house in order . . . Lady Bonham-Carter was quick to realise the terrible shortage of nurses in the Island and threw herself heart and soul into the training of more women . . . She raised V.A. detachments and arranged with the military hospital to give a month's training to the volunteers so that they might have at least some practical experience. Many of us took that month's training, and very kind Imtarfa was to us, for our inexperience must have been a sore trial to sisters and orderlies. We were very grateful for that little bit of training in the years to follow.

"Ships came and went but there was no longer a great fleet in the harbours for any length of time and more and more the Navy concentrated further East. Wives realised that their husbands were unlikely to be in Malta again and gradually drifted homewards." The *Oronsay* carried many women and children back to England.

It has been said that the Maltese people were indifferent to these and other preparations. That is not true. They were calm, which is

3

something other. And unostentatiously the preparations went on. Retired naval officers (as in Aden where I was then serving) were recalled, many of them from farms in Kenya. One was placed in charge of transport, another looked after building and engineering materials, and a large staff was employed in dealing with contraband cargoes.

"A young Australian, a Paymaster Lieutenant on the staff of Vice-Admiral, Malta, Admiral Ford, was lent as assistant to the Government. Besides being the brain behind other departments of defence it was his brilliant organisation and untiring energy which were responsible for the complete stocking of the island for a two year siege. He combined a wide view and amazing foresight with a genius for the minutest detail.

"I have often wondered whether if we had husbanded the supplies we had laid in a little more carefully we should not have survived the whole three years without hunger."

The 'young Australian' who contributed so fruitfully to Malta's ability to survive is now Commander Sir Robert Jackson, K.C.V.O., C.M.G., O.B.E., one of the chief planners of schemes to help the developing countries at United Nations Headquarters. Mrs Norman had spotted a winner.

The fall of France in 1940 wholly transformed the situation, specially for Malta. For one thing, the north African coast, from Tunisia to the Atlantic Ocean instead of providing a chain of secure and friendly harbours, became a hostile bastion overnight. Cape Bon is less than two hundred miles from Malta, and is actually to the north of it. Then came the crucial question, would Italy strike? Some months before, the Italian consul in Aden had told me of his country's war plans. Italy, he said, would enter the war in only one case, and that was, if France were to be on the verge of defeat: then Italy would intervene 'to save France', by a little protective occupation. That is exactly what now happened; only Mussolini overreached himself. He declared war on England as well, an act of arrogant folly which was to cost him not only his colonial empire—he had only to keep his mouth shut to preserve it entire including Abyssinia—but eventually the invasion of his country and finally his own life. But before that sorry consummation was reached, Malta was to suffer grievous perils and wounds at Fascist hands. Mussolini declared war on the 10th June, 1940. For Malta the real war started at dawn next day.

3

MALTA AT WAR

June 1940

The finishing touches had been put to what must always remain an unfinished picture. Young women, Maltese and English, had been enrolled as cypher-clerks; the barbed wire on the beaches had been reinforced, even the milestones had been defaced, lest they enlighten a bewildered invader, even the localities of firms were obliterated on commercial vehicles. Outside the Harbour area, it is these milestones, still staring dumbly from the roadside that nowadays constitute almost the only reminder of the war. They give the wayfarer or rambler quite a shock.

"There had been a flutter of activity among army wives," writes Mrs Norman. "They had heard that they were to be sent home at six hours notice. You must understand that army wives are part of the regiment, they have rations and quarters, their journeys are paid for and arranged and they come very much under War Office orders. As far as the Admiralty is concerned Naval wives are just indiscretions and we are accustomed to have to fend for ourselves, to turn up when needed or vanish when we are in the way."

For the army wives, the six hours' notice was cancelled by the new Governor, General Dobbie. (At first, until Sir Charles Bonham-Carter's definitive retirement, Dobbie was Acting Governor, or Officer Administering the Government as he is officially styled.) He had brought his own wife with him, and had sent for his daughter: the army's women were to stand by their men. The poor Naval wives: they were treated far more brusquely. "One day came an order to Naval wives, repeated at constant intervals all over the island by loud speakers. We were so unused to being catered for that we knew that this must be something really important. Wives whose husbands were in seagoing ships were to leave the island next day in a liner specially set aside to take them to England. 'This is an order and must be obeyed,' repeated the loud speakers again and again." The Slave Ship, as it was inevitably dubbed, sailed the next day and reached port without incident. Wives whose husbands held shore appointments could do as they wished. They all stayed. They were 'offered' quarters in St George's barracks, out on the sea coast beyond St Julian's. "We were feeling very disgruntled at leaving our comfortable homes, but glad to see other families had not left in the exodus.

"Strewn about the barrack grounds were funny little long shaped mounds—the slit trenches that were to be our shelter. I had an almost irresistible temptation to decorate each one of them with one of those large glass bulbs full of white artificial flowers and R.I.P. The place looked discouragingly like a cemetery."

The quarters were dirty, but these gallant ladies turned to and soon had them spick and span. "My husband was not able to come as far as St George's to see me, so once we had made our room ready we decided to move back to our house and have a last few happy days of home life. It lasted just about a week."

In Valetta, the news of Mussolini's declaration of war naturally caused some misgiving. "On Monday evening, 10th June, 1940", writes Mr Emmanuel S. Tonna, M.B.E., now Commandant of the Civil Defence School, in his book *First Focus on Floriana* (1967), "I happened to be in Valetta. The news had just been given on the radio that Italy had joined the armed conflict as the ally of Nazi Germany. As a result there was much commotion in town; many a group of men clashed with the police in trying to ransack certain places well known for their sympathy with the Fascist cause." This last sentence is of great interest and value: it shows how fruitless had been the propaganda campaign of Fascist Italy, and throws into all the more poignant relief the tiny minority, only a few score, whose dissent will be related later on. Among the victims of the popular anger was a wall plaque to Fortunato Mizzi, a former pro-Italian Nationalist of whom a bust had recently, much to the disgust of the majority of Maltese, been unveiled in the 'garden of heroes' on the Pincio in Rome. Today, it is pleasant to record, the plaque is back again in pristine dignity.

"That same evening many families left the harbour areas in search of safer districts; others joined their families in rural localities away from likely target areas, but the majority of the Maltese people stayed put in their homes, hoping for the best. Theirs was naturally a sleepless night!

"I had already joined the Special Constabulary, and the Floriana S.C. were called together at the local Police Station for the necessary briefing. One could notice their anxiety; their inner feelings were reflected on their pale faces—their hour of trial was at hand!

"All those attached to the A.R.P. were expecting a gas raid. Since the Abyssinian Campaign in 1935, Respirator Drill was the order of the day and before retiring to bed many an A.R.P. man tried on his respirator in case.

"Many also had a quick glance at the instructions contained in the booklet, so popular at the time, on *Medical Aspects of Chemical Warfare* by Prof. A. V. Bernard, O.B.E., M.D. (then Chief Government Medical Officer) and *Respirator Drill*, the text used at the Civil Anti-Gas School, Corradino.

"Nothing happened that night and nothing was expected to happen at least before midnight when the Italian ultimatum was to become effective.

"Tuesday 11th June dawned. It was just another day in the calendar, but what an ominous day for Malta. The weather was typical June weather, bright and warm. Life was as usual, except that the schools had closed down, but the ordinary routine was followed with many private terrors and quivering nerves expecting an enemy attack. I like many others belonging to the teaching profession had no hurry to leave home early to catch the bus for school and was caught indoors when the first alarm of an impending raid was given.

"This was at 7 a.m. and immediately our A.A. defences went into action. The barrage was terrific and frightening—never heard before. The people had to huddle themselves beneath staircases, under alcoves and in basements stifling quietly their fear whilst the bombs whistled down. This kind of protection was in accordance with the instructions given out at the time, as underground rock shelters were almost non-existent and high explosive warfare had been almost ruled out in favour of a gas attack."

This sounds almost incredible, but Mr Tonna's testimony (and no-one was in a better position to judge than he was) is supported by so many others. British intelligence was hopelessly at fault, and Malta was to suffer for it. One man had been wiser—Lord Strickland. He had advised the preparation of deep shelters five years earlier, but his counsel went unheeded. Nevertheless, he provided his own newspaper headquarters with a great bell-shaped pit carved out of the rock, as a result of which his newspaper, then edited by his daughter Mabel, appeared every single morning throughout the war.

"The first raid did, however, bring those responsible to their senses, when HE bombs were dropped over Pietà, Floriana and Lower Valetta, with no startling consequences as the number of raiders was very limited and the bombs were not of a very heavy calibre. One of the places hit was the Marina at Pietà, and many a brass hat rushed to the scene after the raid to assess the damage. Experts were heard saying that this was HE Warfare and that the Malta type of building afforded resistance to blast. Householders were, therefore, to be advised to use scantlings to strut the ceilings of basements and seek shelter therein. The timber merchants made a roaring business selling wooden planks and scantlings for the purpose.

"The first raid was over and others followed in quick succession that same morning but with no alarming results. However there was hectic movement on the main roads with people leaving Valetta and Floriana to seek refuge with others away from towns. The Floriana Old Railway Tunnel became alive all of a sudden and it was transformed into a most popular rendezvous for all those who had nowhere to go. Many took up residence there and did not leave before the end of the war over Malta."

"The last adventure of the day came that same evening when there was a concentrated attack over Cospicua at dusk. A nice proportion of high explosives mingled with incendiaries were dropped over this dockyard area, leaving in their wake much devastation and many casualties. Whilst the A.R.P. personnel under their Superintendent, Mr Joseph Storace, were struggling to control the situation, many survivors struggled out of Cospicua in search of safety elsewhere.

"Many refugees from the stricken areas converged upon Floriana. They came in private cars, in cabs, by buses and even on foot – they were all heading towards the same direction – the Old Railway Tunnel which by nightfall was full to capacity.

"Then arose the question of feeding, clothing and bedding – the exodus from Cospicua only brought with them a bundle of bare essentials – no food, no water and no other commodities were immediately available for them. However the band of determined workers, mostly A.R.P. and Special Constables, looked after the refugees as best they could. Through their initiative and fine example they managed to:—

> Cleanse the stuff'd bosom of that perilous stuff
> That weighs upon the heart."

I asked my old friend Mr George Grech, who now lives with his family in Detroit, what he could remember of those days. He replied, with typical Maltese warmth, "It has been so long I could hardly remember that we were in such a mess. But I sure remember when you sent us some sugar and it arrived in the real time. I do remember I shared it with my Mother and my in-laws and it was 'God sent' that is what my dear Mom said and that was true . . . Regarding bombing we lost our houses twice and we didn't have any forks, knives, spoons or other cutlery left. After all who needed those things we really had no use for them. Oh I also remember when the Italians bombed Malta for the first time on 11th June, 1940. I sure remember that at 7 a.m. my wife and I were having fried fresh fish for breakfast when out of a sudden we heard roars of aircraft flying low and we thought they were ours until we heard the guns roar and the bombs blast. We grabbed our three daughters and we did not know what to do. If we go out we might get hurt from bombs, and if we stay in we might get buried under the debris, so we decided to go under the arches of a front window, we did not know what to do we were sure scared. Then in the evening I sent Carrie and daughters to Mellieha with her sister. I stayed home and took care of myself. I used to go and visit them every weekend. That lasted for about three months until shelters were built at Msida. It did not take us long to get used to the falling bombs and the A.A. guns. Such things were not new for us, the Maltese. I remember I used to have my ear-drums blasted with those petard-blasts almost all summer long (Fiestas)."

One of the most vivid descriptions of Malta in her direst hour was given in a broadcast on the 29th June, 1943, by Mrs Queenie Lee, who had lately returned from Malta.

"My husband and I spent four years there, two and a half under war conditions . . . In June 1940 when Italy came into the war, no-one quite knew what to expect. Our first air raid was six hours after war was declared—at dawn on June 11th. There was what seemed then a terrific amount of noise. I didn't know the difference between guns and bombs, as I sat in an old boathouse under some fortifications with other women on war work. We felt comparatively safe as we'd been told it was an air raid shelter and we could sleep there. We were later to learn what safety is—that it's perhaps to be had under sixty feet of rock, but not in an old boathouse. Ours was long ago mixed up with all that was above it. There was excitement in the Island that June, as you'd expect. All the families seemed to think that movement was the solution to all problems. Hundreds and hundreds of them packed up a few possessions and went to seek safety in the centre of the Island, and the squares near the coast and harbour were dead except for battalions of hungry cats. I remember going along the seafront between raids, and seeing no-one but a solitary old man sitting on the edge of a bomb crater, serene in the belief that two bombs never fall in the same place. But our three planes [the famous *Faith*, *Hope* and *Charity*] worked miracles and must have frightened the Italians with their sheer impudence. In a few weeks, raiders were treated with contempt and most people returned to their homes and life became normal except for the inactivity in the creeks and harbour."

There were eight raids in all on that first *dies irae*. As Mr Tonna (known to his friends as Lolly) writes, the first was at 7 a.m. and the last at 7.25 p.m. The airfields were apparently the targets, but the aim of the *Regia Aeronautica* was erratic. No doubt the barrage distracted them. Besides the Army, there was a volunteer anti-aircraft corps in the dockyard. The admiral superintendent had called for volunteers, of whom he wished to enlist four hundred. Five thousand came forward.

Apart from the ground artillery, the only fighter aircraft for the defence of Malta—again this sounds almost unbelievable—were three out-of-date training biplanes, Gloucester Gladiators which were discovered in crates among the stores intended for H.M.S. *Eagle*, herself a veteran of twenty years. Commander Charles Keighley-Peach, the *Eagle*'s Commander (Flying), until he was able to train a few volunteers from his Swordfish pilots, constituted the total fighter force of the fleet. Wounded in the thigh, he nevertheless scored considerable success against the enemy's reconnaissance planes. The three Gladiators were soon christened by the Maltese *Faith*, *Hope* and *Charity*. The skeleton of *Faith* survives to this day in the Palace Armoury, among relics of earlier *gestes* of chivalry.

This day brought its toll of casualties. A bomb fell close to a gun position manned by the Royal Malta Artillery, killing five of its crew. The civilian casualties were seven, three of them being little girls of five, six and seven. A young amateur statistician, Mr Michael Galea, has compiled from official records a list of every single civilian victim from this first day until the last raid in April 1942. (The last alert was sounded on the 28th August, 1944.) This document is invaluable for gauging the relative intensity of the raids. The final tally will be quoted in its place. Meanwhile, we must return to another poignant scene which took place on this momentous day.

Once again, I translate from Sir Arturo Mercieca's autobiography, since he was one of the chief actors in the sad drama. The other was the new Governor, Lieutenant-General William Dobbie, who had succeeded Sir Charles Bonham-Carter, Sir Charles having proceeded on what was technically styled leave, though as Sir Arturo says, all those, including himself, who saw their ailing Governor off, knew that he would never return to Malta. General Dobbie, whom I had met in Palestine, when he arrived in August 1929 in response to Sir Harry Luke's call for troops to quell the communal riots which had broken out, was a man of great piety, a Plymouth Brother. Of him Admiral Cunningham has written that he was "a splendid selection. An Ironside of a man, his profound faith in the justice of our cause and the certainty of Divine assistance made a great impression on the highly religious Maltese. The calm and complete faith shown in the broadcasts he made nearly every evening contributed immensely towards keeping up the morale of the people." As true a tribute as ever was penned.

"On the morning of this first day of the war with Italy," writes Sir Arturo, "while I was at St Paul tat-Targia about to proceed to the city for the usual session of the Criminal Court, I received a telephone message inviting me to call on the Officer Administering the Government at 9.30. I put off the sitting, and went to the city. It was 10.30 before I was able to reach the Palace, I having twice been compelled on the way to take cover from air raids.

"I found the Governor who was waiting for me, and with him the Lieutenant-Governor, Sir Edward Jackson. General Dobbie, without any preamble, told me he had received from the Secretary of State for the Colonies instructions to invite me to signify my resignation from the office of Chief Justice and President of the Court of Appeal on account of my pro-Italian sympathies and the existence of a state of war with Italy. He added that on the fifth of that month an Order had been issued by the King in Council authorising the Secretary of State to order my removal from office, despite any provision to the contrary in other laws, in the event of my not resigning voluntarily. In either case I was to receive the whole of the pension due to me. He concluded by asking me to give him the requisite answer, if possible that morning.

"I asked to see the Order in Council to which he had referred. After examining it, I answered that having ascertained that as far as

I was concerned there had been withdrawn the guarantees of my independence as a judge, which consisted in being irremovable from office for any reason whatever except proven turpitude or incapacity, I had no way open to me except to resign from my post. I asked moreover for permission to make public my letter of resignation, and to make reference in it to the Order in Council of the 5th June. The Governor after consulting Jackson, said that there was no objection.

"He then informed me that he was constrained to impose certain restrictions on my personal liberty, and on that of my wife and my two children, Victor and Lilian, but that we might stay on in our summer residence at Naxxar. I then affirmed my faith in the rights of the Italian culture and language, which I had always openly upheld as a deputy of the people, as a civil servant and also as a judge, when giving evidence before the Royal Commission. I ended my declaration with a protest against my being deprived of the guarantees to which I was entitled as one of the judges of His Majesty.

"Having drafted then and there my letter of resignation, I handed it to General Dobbie. In bidding me farewell, he offered me his hand saying: 'I don't know if I'm doing wrong; but personally I know nothing against you.' I replied: 'Be assured that you are shaking the hand of a gentleman.' "

Inter arma silent leges, in wartime the law is silent: it was a brutal Roman who first uttered this brutal maxim. It must be remembered that the Island lay under the threat of an invasion, and that, guided and warned by what had already taken place in other parts of Europe, the Government simply could not risk the emergence of any 'quislings'. With Sir Arturo, therefore, a number of others of known Italian sympathies were arrested and then interned. They were perhaps eighty all told. General Dobbie humanely placed them in the charge of one of their fellow-countrymen to whose nature any sort of harshness is utterly foreign, the present Major Walter Bonello. I have before me the diary of one of them, which shows that they were permitted considerable latitude, and were allowed to maintain contact with their families. Early in 1942 all the political detainees, except thirteen, were transported to Kenya, whence they were repatriated in groups during the last months of 1944 and the beginning of 1945.

It is a sad story, especially in retrospect. These men were not criminals, nor spies. No charge was ever brought against them. They were victims. The most intelligent of them, who is a friend of mine, has told me that they underwent no cruelty, and very seldom any unkindness. They were honest men with the courage of their convictions; and it was those convictions that convicted them. Looking back on this sorry, shabby affair, one can only find comfort in three things: that those affected were so few—about eighty, my friend says; secondly that they were treated so courteously, and thirdly that so many of them survive to be admired citizens and ornaments of the international society of contemporary Malta.

4

ACTIVE AND PASSIVE

1940

After the first days of war, the inhabitants of Malta, military no less than civilian, found themselves puzzled less by what had happened than (like Sherlock Holmes on a famous occasion) by what had not. First, there had been no gas-attacks, which meant that all the precautions taken, and training bestowed during the preceding three years went for naught. A wholly new pattern of defence and habitation must by improvised. Secondly, although Malta had been 'written off' before the war by the Chiefs of Staff as indefensible, the expected invasion had not occurred, and never did occur.

To enlarge upon the former point, let us again quote Mr Tonna. "When the war started there were no rock shelters in Floriana except the Railway Tunnel extending from the Old Railway Station in Valetta right through to Porte des Bombes. A good stretch of this Tunnel ran beneath the Rundle Gardens, the Mall and the Argotti and hence the people of Floriana had ample space where to seek refuge in the event of air-raids.

"On the outbreak of hostilities there was, however, an outcry for more shelter space in other parts of Floriana and, in no time, the suburb was honeycombed with underground excavations. Had not this project been completed in good time many people would have paid the supreme sacrifice during the blitz on Floriana in 1942.

"People were very much encouraged to dig cubicles at their own expense both in the underground shelters and on the face of the bastion walls—the latter are still visible in the bastions lying in the Porte des Bombes area and in the Orange Grove beneath St Anne's Curtain, Floriana.

"To dig a private cubicle in a public rock shelter one had to ask permission from the District Commissioner which was invariably granted provided one would give an undertaking in writing to bind oneself to the following conditions: the work must be completed within three months and the tunnelling must be level with the rest of the shelter. Cubicles had to be no more than six feet wide and no doors were to be fixed. A right of way was also to be allowed through any part of the shelter dug voluntarily. An encroachment fee of one shilling per annum was to be paid." This must be one of the oddest forms of lease ever drawn up for the use of Government property.

"It was a very expensive enterprise to dig a private shelter for the exclusive use of one's own family but it was a worthwhile undertaking. Our family shelter was beneath the Argotti (the Royal Malta University Botanical Gardens) in Gnien is-Sultan. In the same area there were three others belonging to Mr C. Penza, Mr J. Agius and our uncle, Mr Gaetano Busuttil (RIP). Late in the evenings we all used to gather together and recite the Holy Rosary before retiring for the night. We were like one big family and the fact that the shelter was away from the hubbub of the suburb was to me a real place of refuge and where one could have a good night's rest. The four cubicles were connected with each other to allow for blast escape.

"Reverting to public shelters the system of voluntary shelter supervisors did not work satisfactorily with the exception of a few who really felt their responsibility. Very prominent amongst these few was the Very Rev. Canon Publius Farrugia, the Dean of the Chapter of St Paul's Shipwreck Church in Valetta who agreed to be Shelter Supervisor at the public shelter beneath the School. Dun Pupull as he was affectionately known, used to exercise very strict discipline and his own private cubicle was a model, being very neat and well organised. I distinctly remember the day when Dun Pupull came to me, in full consternation, to report that the case of tinned milk I had given him for some emergency use, had been stolen from his cubicle whilst he was on a tour of the shelter.

"Many similar thefts had occurred but the most daring one was when the entire emergency stock of foodstuffs was lifted from the shelter beneath the Argotti. The store in the shelter used to be properly locked and the key was kept with me; however those who stole the entire consignment were more clever, as they brought it out through the ventilation hole which was large enough for the foodstuff cases to be pulled out through.

"Each night I used to visit different shelters in turn and many a time I was assailed by the people with all sorts of complaints. I could not do otherwise but listen. In the majority of cases the complaints were justified but redress was impossible as I had not the facilities nor the provisions to accommodate the people's wishes.

"I know of three large public shelters in Floriana which were mostly excavated by voluntary labour: the one under the London Confectionery extending to the Lion Fountain in St Anne's Square; the one beneath the Seminary which was connected with the one in the Argotti and the one in Gunlayer Square which almost received a direct hit on Sunday 1st March, 1942 when several persons were killed. Volunteers also offered their services in the installation of electric light."

Mr Tonna concludes this graphic description of life in Malta's Second Neolithic Age with the following:

"I want to finish this reminiscence by quoting the prayer which used to be recited during the war in shelters during air-raids.

OUR HOPE IN THE LORD

Bless this shelter Lord we pray
During Air Raids night and day.
Bless the people here within,
Keep them safe and free from sin.

Bless the gunners as they work,
The searchlights guide when dangers lurk.
Bless each chasing Aircraft crew,
Lend Thine aid to all they do.

Bless the members of Thy flock,
Keep them free from Air Raid shock;

Bless the light and keep it bright
And away from aliens sight.

Bless our wardens one and all
Answering to their country's call;
Our Gallant firemen, help them Lord,
Let Thy grace be their reward.

Bless all those who work for PEACE
That hostilities may cease.

Nihil obstat Datum Melitae die 17 Januarii 1941
P. Adeodatus M. Schembri O.S.A. Censor Theol."

All quarrymen and miners were ordered to register with Government, in order that they might be employed as usefully as possible. The water department erected standpipes in areas most thickly frequented by refugees, and electricity was installed where necessary. The Royal Navy as was to be expected had taken its own measures in good time. A vast tunnel had been excavated down by the dockyard, and this provided shelter for a thousand labourers, besides officers and their families. This, I am told, was due to the personal initiative of Mr Malcolm MacDonald, at that time Secretary of State for the Colonies.

As for the invasion, it was expected to come either from the sea or the sky or both. A special anti-parachute section of the Police was formed. Knowing what we now do about the Italian naval strategy, and that its supreme object was to avoid contact with the Royal Navy, it is not hard to understand the Italian reluctance to engage in any sort of seaborne adventure against Malta. Nor in those days was the *Regia Aeronautica* trained to carry out an airborne invasion.

But in the words of Mrs Norman, "our really shattering thunderclap was the news of the fall of France (on the 24th June). A Fleet and Air Force were at once lost to our aid. The sea, which was our only lifeline became at once a narrow channel, infested with mines and submarines and within the range now of enemy airfields all the

4

way from Gibraltar to Malta. Nine hundred miles to eastward, nine hundred miles to westward were our nearest points of contact with British held shores . . ."

Just what Malta's rôle was to be was shown early in July. On the 7th of that month, Cunningham had put to sea in order to protect two convoys which were taking the wives and children of servicemen from Malta to Alexandria and also stores for the fleet. Cunningham was the exact opposite of the Italian high command. 'Attack and destroy' was his motto. I well remember my first meeting with him. It was in 1934, when I first arrived in Malta. I had met again Charles Lambe (who died in 1960 as Admiral of the Fleet Sir Charles Lambe, First Sea Lord). We had been friends at Cambridge, eleven years before. Charles was at that time a Commander on the staff of 'A.B.C.', as he was known. He said to me one day: "Of course, you'll be calling on all the admirals, and I'm sure you'll like them, too. But there's one man who really counts, and that's my boss, Cunningham, I must take you to see him." At that time there were indeed many admirals in Malta, and they were a most likeable lot. Almost at the bottom of the flag-list was Andrew Cunningham, at that time Rear-Admiral, Destroyers, known as 'R.A.D.' The moment Charles introduced me to him, I realised why Charles, and a group of his co-evals, all of whom were to become outstanding sailors during the war, all said "A.B.C.'s the man. Watch him, he'll go right to the top." He did. There was about him a kind of quiet power, a sort of perpetual movement of spirit, which shone from his bright kind eyes. This man, 'the greatest sailor since Nelson' was now in command in the Mediterranean.

On the afternoon of the 8th July, after repeated air attacks which did remarkably little damage, Cunningham learned that the Italian fleet was at sea. His own battleships were slower than the Italians but he could hope to bring them to action if he could get between them and their base at Taranto, whither he at once steered. After a preliminary air skirmish, soon after 3 p.m. the two fleets came in sight of each other. The British fleet was heavily outgunned, as well as outpaced, by the Italian; nevertheless, as soon as the *Warspite* had scored one hit on the enemy's flagship, Admiral Campioni turned away under a smoke-screen. During the next four days repeated air attacks were made on the British squadron, but with hardly a hit registered. The fleet's anti-aircraft gunnery was ineffective, but the Gladiators from the *Eagle* flown by Charles Keighley-Peach and two volunteers from the Swordfish squadrons, brought down five enemy bombers—"a score which was later to rise to eleven, showing" in Macintyre's words "what might be accomplished by a proper fighter defence." The safe arrival of the two convoys at Alexandria brought the operation to an end.

The action was not of cardinal importance in itself; but Macintyre's comment on it is of great value for an understanding of Malta's wartime strategic rôle:

"It set the pattern for much that was to happen in the future. It also clearly presented the problem facing the two antagonists in the Mediterranean, though it cannot be said that either fully understood it.

"To both it demonstrated that a British fleet operating from Alexandria could not prevent the safe passage of Italian supply convoys to Africa. From the Italian point of view this supported their contention that there was nothing to be gained from sending their battle-fleet out to seek action as an end in itself. What the Italians failed to see was that this situation must sooner or later force the British to strain every nerve to restore Malta—written off before the war by the Chiefs of Staff as indefensible—as an air and naval base from which to attack their convoys to Libya. The only certain way to prevent this was by capturing it while it yet lay virtually defenceless. This the Italian Navy had urged on the Italian *Commando Supremo*. General Rommel was to do the same when appointed to command the Afrika Korps, offering to command the operation himself. But both the Italian and German Supreme Commands believed they could achieve their object merely by neutralising the island by air attack. It was to prove a fatal mistake."

It was, but what a year of grinding anxiety 1940 was. England was alone. France had turned to malignant collaboration. The British army had been utterly disorganised at Dunkirk. Norway, Denmark, Holland and Belgium—all had fallen before the Nazis. England herself was in jeopardy. The Battle of Britain had yet to be fought and won. In Malta there was still no adequate fighter strength. Of the Island's three airfields one was not finished, and no attempt had been made even to provide pens for the planes by the sides of the runways.

There had been a general call-up and a Home Guard had been formed. Both the Island's regiments, the Royal Malta Artillery, and the territorial King's Own Malta Regiment were expanded, the latter enlisting almost two whole companies from former Boy Scouts. Steps were taken to prevent hoarding, or spreading false rumours. Stray dogs and cats were destroyed. In July an attempt was made to turn the basements and cellars of the more strongly-built houses into shelters, but this proved what one of the Protection Officers styled 'a grand fiasco'. The Maltese preferred the deep shelters, such as the 'popular rendezvous' of the old Tunnel. Agriculture was stimulated, and the golf course and polo-grounds put under crops.

A Special Constabulary was raised. Five thousand volunteers came forward. This was a move of much wisdom; because a large proportion of those who offered their services were teachers, and as such more in touch with the inhabitants than men of other callings. They knew their families, and, which was of the greatest value, the parish priests who played so vital a part in sustaining the morale of the inhabitants.

Eventually the corps was divided into two, one section becoming the equivalent of the British Home Guard. They were employed as 'spotters' against possible parachutists. They were instructed to report with such arms as they possessed. These were sporting guns for the most part, some even being old muzzle-loaders.

The adjutant of the Specials was Mr Philip Pullicino of the Lieutenant-Governor's Office, a member of a distinguished family whose father, Sir Philip Pullicino, was at that time Attorney-General. Mr Pullicino later became commandant of the Specials, and so effective were his services that in 1942 the Commissioner of Police and the members of his Force presented him on the occasion of his marriage with a fine silver salver inscribed with an expression of their gratitude. It now adorns the drawing-room of the Malta embassy in Rome, where Mr Pullicino is accredited to the Quirinal.

The Specials saw active service, too. One evening a bomb fell on the enclosed convent of the Benedictine nuns in Mdina. Mr Pullicino whose family home is in that city, was by good fortune in the neighbourhood and was soon on the spot, together with a lady A.R.P. warden. The godly inhabitants of the convent at first refused entrance to anyone; but eventually, faced with the possibility of a forced entrance they admitted Mr Pullicino and an R.A.F. pilot who had appeared on the scene—but not the lady A.R.P. warden. A frightened nun preceded the rescuers, and as she proceeded down the corridor ringing her bell, the nuns hurried off into their cells. The bomb had demolished the top storey of the convent, and had precipitated two nuns in their beds onto the floor below. One of them, a very old lady, died almost immediately, and it fell to the rescue-party to have her corpse reverently conveyed to the chapel of the Convent.

Mr Pullicino has told me how amazingly efficient the ground barrage was. "It worked with push-button precision," he said. As soon as the alert was given, every gun in every battery in the Island concentrated its fire on the target indicated, be it the Harbour or one of the airfields. Not long ago Mr Pullicino met the retiring chief of the Italian Air Staff. He asked him whether he knew Malta. "Yes, but only from the air." He had been a fighter-pilot in many a raid over Malta, and he recollected how deadly that barrage had been.

The raids continued, there were more than two hundred in 1940—the destruction spread. Military casualties were few, fewer than a hundred civilians had lost their lives. Malta had settled down to war conditions. At first, social life continued. There were dances at the clubs, cinemas remained open, but to economise electricity current was supplied only to the projection-rooms: the houses remained dark, and the spectators had to grope their way in and out. Bars were still frequented, prices rising as stocks dwindled.

Cheering messages had been received from the English Cabinet, from the Lords Commissioners of the Admiralty. General Dobbie constantly broadcast to the people, taking them into his confidence, and invoking the assistance of the Almighty. (A friend has told me that General Dobbie used to consult her on the composition of these talks, and particularly asked her to put in the references to God in the appropriate places.) Malta's defences had been slightly augmented. Cunningham even before the war had pressed for the Island's air defence to be built up, but in vain. Shortly before the fall of France *Faith*, *Hope* and *Charity*, still flown by spare flying-boat pilots, were reinforced by five Hurricanes, which had reached Malta via France and Tunis. Although the Air Officer Commanding Mediterranean appealed in August for a modest fifteen aircraft, all Malta received for offensive sorties, was No 830 Squadron of the Fleet Air Arm, nine Swordfish which had originally been based on Toulon to co-operate with the French Navy. The ground defences should have by now comprised 112 heavy and sixty light guns: in fact they amounted to thirty-four heavy and eight light. There was one radar set, and that could not work all the time.

What a paradox: the English made Malta an easy prey for an Italian invader; the Italians failed to attempt to seize it. Meanwhile Malta was being reinforced. Twelve Hurricane fighters were flown into Malta from the carrier *Argus* on 12th August. On the 1st September the first convoy of the war, three merchant ships and a tanker, reached Malta. The citizens manned the sea-fronts and battlements to welcome and cheer. Another convoy followed early in October, a third in the last days of November. By the end of September, also, 2,000 troops, conveyed in naval vessels had arrived to reinforce Malta's garrison. Most important of all was the increase in air-strength. On the 1st September, the new aircraft carrier, the *Illustrious*, which was provided with an armoured flight-deck, joined Cunningham's fleet for the opening of what was to be a spectacular shooting-season. It was Swordfish aircraft from the *Illustrious* which were to cripple the Italian battle-fleet at Taranto. This great feat of arms was made possible by the presence in Malta of No 431 Flight of the R.A.F. consisting of three Glen-Martin 'Maryland' reconnaissance aircraft. They were fast, and climbed high. They could, and did, range far and wide over the Mediterranean, which the Sutherland flying-boats based on the Island could not do, and so were able to keep a watch on Italian harbours, including Taranto.

As though to mark the end of an epoch, on the 22nd August the death had occurred of Lord Strickland. He was seventy-eight. For more than fifty years this remarkable and gifted man had fought for the rights of the Maltese people and the Maltese language as he saw them. He will always be reckoned among the greatest of Malta's sons.

Had his advice been heeded, Malta's plight would not have been so dire at his death. Lord Strickland was a resolute exponent of the theory that Malta's destiny was indissolubly linked with that of Great Britain, which he himself had served in several Colonial and Commonwealth governorships, and as a member of the House of Commons, before his elevation to the peerage. He was a Maltese Noble in his own right. He was an implacable adversary of Fascist intrigue and of those of his countrymen who despite it still harboured pro-Italian sympathies.

Much of his energy, his resolution and his fearlessness have been inherited by his daughter Mabel, who did so much to animate her fellow-citizens in those dread days. As the year 1940 closed there was cheering news from the Western desert of Egypt, where General Wavell had set in motion the campaign that was to annihilate an Italian army; but it had been a terrible year for Malta. Malta was now 'in the war' with a vengeance. How was Malta to get out? Not for two more years would the answer to that question be given.

There was however one bright interlude to cheer the last days of the dying year. While the advance in the Western desert continued, Admiral Cunningham decided to revisit Malta, and this is how he describes his return:

"The *Warspite* steamed into the Grand Harbour during the early afternoon of 20th December. It was our first visit since May, and news of our arrival had been spread abroad. As we moved in with our band playing and guard paraded the Barraccas and other points of vantage were black with wildly-cheering Maltese. Our reception was touchingly overwhelming. It was good to know that they realised that though the fleet could not use Malta for the time being, we had them well in mind.

"I went round seeing all our old friends in the intervals of more official visits. Admiralty House looked very stripped and deserted, and in the hall I was met by my bandmaster and our two Maltese maids, both the latter weeping with emotion and asking if I could not persuade my wife to return.

"I went all over the dockyard next morning with the Vice-Admiral and was mobbed by crowds of excited workmen singing 'God Save the King' and 'Rule Britannia'. I had difficulty in preventing myself from being carried around, and had to make more than a dozen impromptu speeches telling all and sundry how greatly the fleet still depended on them, and congratulating them on the fine way they were working under incessant attack and great difficulties. It was a very moving experience, and once again I realised what a great acquisition we had in Sir Wilbraham Ford (Admiral in charge of the dockyard). I had several meetings with the Governor, Lieutenant-General (later Sir) William Dobbie, another fine man and a tower of strength. My staff discussed the supply situation. We stayed in Malta about forty hours completely undisturbed by any air attack. It was a most useful visit."

5

THE OTHER SIDE

1940–41

The year 1941 forms Act Two of the Drama, and 1942 Act Three, with a climax such as few dramatists could have conceived; but before proceeding to attempt a synopsis of them, it will be well to analyse the motives and actions of one of the chief actors in it, namely the enemy.

It happens that we have an abundant source for this in the Official History of the Italian Navy, of which a substantial volume of over 400 pages, with maps, is devoted wholly to Malta. It is called *Operazione C3*: *Malta* and it was published in 1965.

So far as the story has developed to date, three cardinal factors emerge from a study of the Italian history. First, a plan for the invasion and capture of Malta had been drawn up before the war—or rather not so much drawn up as dreamed up. No less than 40,000 troops were to be employed, to be conveyed in flat-bottomed landing craft, and escorted by a considerable fleet. The enterprise was to depend on surprise, and 'a temporary naval superiority' that is, of some forty-eight hours only, before Cunningham could arrive from Alexandria. The main landing was to be made in the bays at the north end of the Island, Mellieha and St Paul's in particular, with a diversionary thrust at Marsaxlok. The Italians estimated that there were in Malta between ten and twelve thousand troops whom it would be necessary to overcome in order to capture it. In addition to the invading army, and the naval escort, no less than 500 aircraft were to supply cover.

Why was this plan never put into effect? The Italian history supplies two perfectly simple answers. The first is that Italy did not possess the necessary resources. The men were not there. The parachutists were not trained. The ships did not exist, the landing-craft were confined to the drawing-board, the air force had nothing like the aircraft requisite for the undertaking. Could they not have been supplied? This brings us to the second answer. When Mussolini declared war, he was gambling. He was no strategist, and no judge of character. He reckoned that France was finished, and that therefore England would hurry to the nearest available conference table. That being so, it was essential that Italy should be there too, to pick up anything that might be going. This was Mussolini's idea of 'the diplomatic war': why fight when talking would do?

Mussolini's attitude both puzzled and disappointed the Germans —and this was to have a decisive effect on future campaigns. The German military attaché in Rome from 1936 to 1943, Von Rintelen, published a book of which the Italian translation appeared in 1952. *Mussolini the Ally* it is called.

"Just before the Italian declaration of war," writes Von Rintelen, "Admiral Canaris wanted to know from me what active measures the Italians intended to take. I could only answer that I knew of none, and that I had the impression that nothing had been prepared. The German high command would hardly credit it, and I in my turn formed the idea that everything had been kept secret." This, comments the Italian history, seemed logical enough in Berlin. Hitler himself had tried to dissuade Mussolini from entering the war prematurely and unprepared. The Duce had wanted to come in on the 5th June. When, despite Hitler's request that he should wait a little longer, until he was in a position to undertake some sort of military action, Mussolini insisted that he could not postpone his declaration of war beyond the 10th, the German High Command naturally thought that "something big was brewing." Von Rintelen himself thought that this view was confirmed by a conversation he had with Mussolini, in which the Duce "explained that he had intended to intervene earlier, from which I deduced that there was in preparation some action against Corsica, Tunis or Malta, which could not be deferred owing to the difficulty of maintaining secrecy.

Thus, I was astounded when on the afternoon of the 10th he gave notice from the balcony of the Palazzo Venezia that from the hour zero of the next day Italy would be in a state of war with the western powers.

"But my expectation that the following morning something would happen was deluded: nothing happened . . . Mussolini, with his unexpected decision to intervene, had omitted to create the necessary conditions precedent for the struggle against Great Britain. Paramount among these was the elimination of the British base of Malta. Italian officials of the Staff told me that the idea of a combined operation, an attack by sea and air, has been discussed between the three Armed Forces, but that it was not followed up as being too difficult."

The Japanese naval attaché, Captain Toyo Mitunobu, formed much the same impression. It may seem odd to quote a Japanese view, but as will be seen, the Japanese did in fact have a definite share in later plans for the humbling of Malta. In an article published in Milan in 1956, entitled "Observations on the war in Italy, 1940–1944", Captain Mitunobu writes: "From my point of view, Italy, by actively intervening in the war, should have been ready to conquer Malta and Tunisia, which are the key points for the control of the Mediterranean. Judging by Italy's domestic propaganda, from the second half of May down to the declaration of war in June 1940, I thought that that would happen immediately after her entry into the war; but Italy declared, on the afternoon of 10th June, that she would enter the war on the morning of 11th June. This surprised me. And then, on the 11th, 12th, 13th and 14th June, operations for the conquest of Malta and Tunis still had not started. This was to me incomprehensible. Perhaps Italy had some reasons for it. . . [the lack, for war in the Mediterranean of] a plan worked out in detail, as well as preparation and the decision to put it into effect from the beginning of the war."

The Italian official history sums up as follows:

"But all those who were looking for a 'blitz-operation' on Malta or on any other objective—at the moment of the Italian intervention, were wrong. Not a single infernal machine went off on the morning of 11th June, for the simple reason that the means were lacking and the men were not prepared. Besides, the inferiority of the Italian navy in face of the Anglo-French in the Mediterranean was so heavy that any initiative against Malta—as against Tunis or Corsica—would have had to be supported by aircraft and parachutists to have any probability of success . . . These conclusions could not fail to take into account, with decisive effect, the political premisses of a short war, on which was founded the decision to throw Italy into the war, and to throw her at that precise moment. In the light of these considerations there appears to be no foundation, from the operational point of view, for the statement in the report of the German military attaché of the 2nd April, 1942, to his headquarters, that the Italian High Command recognised 'the gross error committed in not starting the war with the conquest of Malta.'"

As already noted, logistically any such operation was out of the question. "This being so, it must be admitted that if there was a 'gross error', it really consisted in not having prepared the operation in good time during the days of peace. Above all, an Italian blitz-action would have been of great value whether in view of a short war, for reasons of prestige, or in view of a long war, for the reasons which for years had been so clearly put forward by the navy. On this point—which found everyone or nearly everyone in agreement, Italians, Germans, English, French and Japanese—it is possible to agree."

In the light of these very revealing facts, Malta's rôle in the war becomes of far greater significance. The Island is no longer merely the heroic martyr, though that she was to remain for two more years, she takes on two more capacities. First, Malta becomes the springboard for an ever-mounting offensive against the supply routes of the Axis forces in North Africa, an offensive which in the end proved crippling to them and secondly Malta, far from being the ripe pear as it was hopefully described by Italian dreamers, turned out to be an apple of discord which increasingly soured German-Italian relations. Malta's passive rôle earned, and still commands, universal acclaim; but her active one was to have a decisive share in the outcome of the war.

ACT TWO

6

BLITZ-KRIEG

1941

The Italians borrowed much from the Germans including the word *blitz-krieg*, or lightning-war. They called it *guerra-lampo*, which was not at all the same thing. It sounds, and was, far milder. As already explained, they had abandoned any idea of invading Malta, they relied on what they called 'Sterilisation' or 'Neutralisation' by air —any word would do so long as it sounded fierce enough, and involved no increase in mere action. In fact, the raids became fewer and less effective. The Island's defences had been steadily built up and reinforced throughout the year. Mr Galea's statistics show that of the 210 alerts of 1940, about half of which were followed by bombing attacks, during the second half of the year fatal casualties were mercifully few, twelve in July, none in August, five in September, and then no more. The Greeks had driven the Italians back into Albania by the 6th December, and by the 16th the Italians had been expelled altogether from Egypt by Wavell's brilliant campaign. Wavell was the first, though by no means the last, to prove that in this war, unlike the war of 1914–18, the preponderance of brilliant generalship was on the side of the allies. Wavell had served in Palestine with Allenby, whose biographer he was to be. Shortly before the last war he had headed a military mission to Russia, and had watched the Soviet experiments with parachute troops. Being the man he was he at once saw—and up to that time he was the only foreign soldier to do so—the enormous potentialities of the new arm.

This uneasy peace, for even so it was no more, was soon to be shattered, and 1941 was to be a year of hazards second only to those which were to follow in 1942. Early in the new year it became known that Hitler had despatched part of his air force to help Italy. On Thursday, the 2nd January, it was officially announced in Rome: "On the occasion of the arrival in Italy of some sections of the German Air Force, the chief of the Italian Air Staff, General Pricolo, in a special order of the day, has stated that the German air contingent will participate in the air and naval struggle in the Mediterranean, and it is to be considered as a big Italian unit. The common struggle will consecrate the brotherhood in arms between Italy and Germany."

It was to do a good deal more than that: it was wholly to transform the state of affairs in the Mediterranean war. The proof of this came immediately.

In December, a convoy of four ships had reached Malta, escorted only by the old battleship *Malaya* and four destroyers. During the respite from air attack, the dockyard had been brought back into working order. Malta had even gone over to the offensive, although her air-strength was still lamentably meagre. The fighter defences were still only sixteen Hurricanes. To the original striking-force of twelve naval Swordfish of 830 squadron, only sixteen Wellington bombers had been added. Nevertheless they bombed the harbours of Bari, Brindisi and Taranto, which were the ports whence supplies for Greece were despatched. In Naples harbour, now the chief base of the Italian Navy, a cruiser and a battleship were damaged. For long-range reconnaissance the four Sunderland flying-boats and four Marylands were the sole craft available.

Not long ago the major-domo of the San Anton Palace asked me what I was writing now. When I told him, he at once said, "H.M.S. *Illustrious*". It was this great ship, already the victor of Taranto, which was to be the protagonist in the first trial of strength between Malta and the *Luftwaffe*, so much so that to this day she is regarded as a kind of talisman in Malta. Twenty-eight years later there is still, fronting the Palace Square 'H.M.S. ILLUSTRIOUS BAR, by Mary and Paul'. Her aircraft had already sunk two out of three supply ships making for Tripoli, of which they also attacked the port and its shipping.

After the blitz rubble is removed. The timber will provide precious fuel, the stone a makeshift home, complete with laundry.

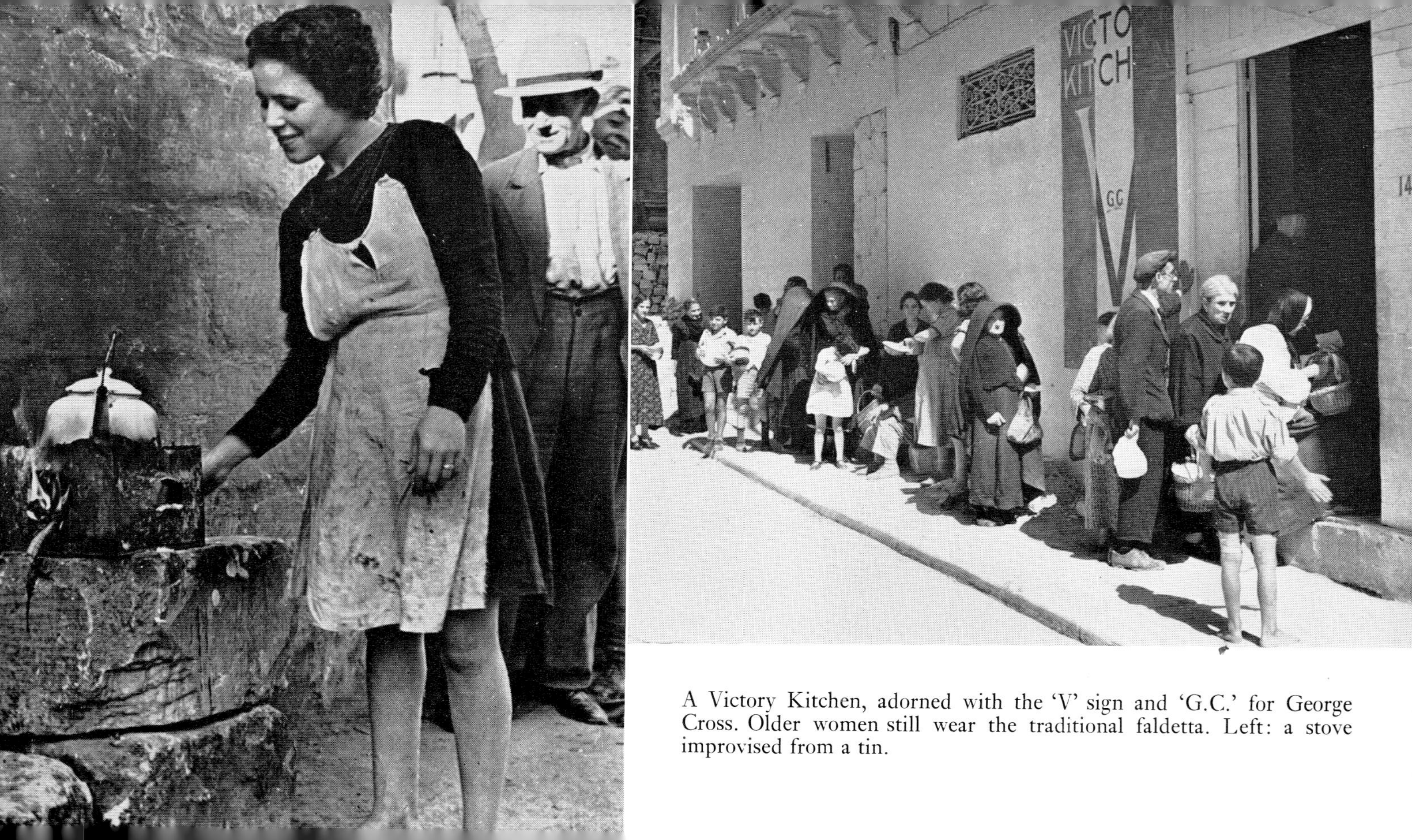

A Victory Kitchen, adorned with the 'V' sign and 'G.C.' for George Cross. Older women still wear the traditional faldetta. Left: a stove improvised from a tin.

Late in December, a grand convoy had been planned, timed to take advantage of the new, relatively safe, conditions. Five ships, of which one contained 4,000 tons of ammunition, twelve Hurricanes in crates, and 3,000 tons of seed potatoes for Malta, and four vessels destined for Piraeus, were to sail east from Gibraltar. At the same time two laden ships for Malta and two convoys of empties, starting from Alexandria, were to be protected by cruisers. Cunningham with his carrier and two battleships was to go ahead to meet the convoy from the west in the Sicilian channel.

Had the original time-table been adhered to, 'Operation Excess' as it was code-named, might well have reached its goal without incident, instead of providing the still-remembered saga which it actually did. The ships sailed on time, together with a large convoy which was to go via the Cape, from which the Malta-bound vessels were to break away when they reached the latitude of Gibraltar. But on Christmas Day the appearance of the German cruiser *Hipper* forced the convoy to scatter, while ships were sent out from Gibraltar to come to its assistance. Then, in heavy weather, the old battleship *Renown* was damaged by the raging waves, and had to retire to Gibraltar for repairs. Finally one of the transports destined for Greece was driven ashore by the gale. Thus it came about that only on the 6th January were the four remaining transports and their escort, known as Force H, able to sail from Gibraltar. The delay was fatal, for it provided the German *Fliegercorps* X time to install itself on the airfields of Sicily. This detachment was a crack unit. It was manned by pilots who had gained valuable experience over Norway and England; and it was armed with the deadly Junkers 87's (Stukas), that is true dive-bombers, which could plummet vertically from the sky to drop their 1,000 lb. bombs with lethal accuracy. This was their Mediterranean début.

On the 27th December, 1940, General Geissler, who commanded this crack 'CAT X' (Corpo Aereo Tedesco, or German Air Corps) as it was known, had come to an agreement with the Italian High Command in Rome that the tasks of the German Air Force in the Mediterranean should be as follows:

(a) To attack enemy maritime traffic, in collaboration with the Italian Air Force;
(b) To attack the bases at Alexandria and Malta;
(c) To plant mines in the Suez Canal and in the approaches to the nearer enemy ports.

The Italians made but little effort to intervene with their navy. In fact, when on the night of the 8th January, a few Wellingtons from Malta, now an offensive base, raided Naples, they damaged the battleship *Cesare*, one of the two Italian battleships which had survived Taranto, whereupon both the *Cesare* and the *Vittor io Veneto* were at once withdrawn to Genoa, thus leaving the British sea-lanes completely unmolested. But not so the skies.

At first it looked as though the Italian attack would be delivered with its usual operatic bravura, ten Savoia 79's showering, but not hitting, the *Malaya* and *Gloucester*, and losing two of their numbers to Fulmars from the *Ark Royal* just before Force H turned back towards Gibraltar. That was at dusk on 9th January. At dawn on the 10th the convoy had come under the protection of Cunningham's main force, the two battleships *Warspite* and *Valiant*, the *Illustrious* and five destroyers. His cruisers, the *Gloucester*, *Southampton* and *Bonaventure* were escorting the destroyer *Gallant* which had struck a mine and was being towed to Malta by the *Mohawk*. "It seemed", says Macintyre, "that the operation—the most ambitious and complex convoy operation so far attempted—was achieving complete success. An Italian reconnaissance plane was chopped out of the sky with deadly efficiency by Fulmars from the *Illustrious*." On the preceding day a force of Italian bombers and fighters had failed to locate Cunningham, nor had sporadic attacks by bombers and torpedo planes on the convoy had the slightest effect. This Italian reconnaissance plane therefore was the forlorn hope of the *Regia Aeronautica*. It too failed, yet another victim to the *Illustrious*. It is easy to comprehend how the *Illustrious* now wore an aura of baneful majesty in the eyes of the Italians—and of their German allies.

At 1.30 p.m., while the Fulmars on patrol were chasing away two Italian torpedo planes, a great host of aircraft was seen approaching, squadron by squadron, from the north. These were the famous Stukas, the genuine dive-bombers. Behind them came the Junkers 88, which carried a heavier load of bombs, and approached to the attack at a more oblique angle. Against them the slow-mounting Fulmars could do but little.

"We opened up with every A.A. gun we had as one by one the Stukas peeled off into their dives," writes Cunningham, "concentrating almost the whole venom of their attack upon the *Illustrious.* At times she became almost completely hidden in a forest of great bomb splashes". The next sentences are typical of their writer. "One was too interested", Cunningham goes on, "in this new form of dive-bombing attack to be frightened, and there was no doubt we were watching complete experts. Formed roughly in a large circle over the fleet they peeled off one by one when reaching the attacking position. We could not but admire the skill and precision of it all. The attacks were pressed home to point blank range, and as they pulled out of their dives some of them were seen to fly along the flight deck of the *Illustrious* below the level of her funnel.

"I saw her hit early on just before the bridge, and in all, in something like ten minutes, she was hit by six 1,000 lb. bombs, to leave the line badly on fire, her steering gear crippled, her lifts out of action, and with heavy casualties . . .

"The *Illustrious* reported herself as badly hit and making for Malta; but it was not until 3.30 p.m. that she was steering more or less steadily in that direction at seventeen knots." What an amazing feat of seamanship it was. It was her armoured flight-deck which had saved her, the skill of her captain which enabled her to be steered on her engines alone. "Between four and five o'clock", Cunningham continues, "still on fire, she was attacked, with the battleships, by another twenty-five dive-bombers. My heart sank as I watched her, wondering how with all her heavy damage, she would stand up to it. I need not have worried. As the attacks developed I saw every gun in the *Illustrious* flash into action, a grand and inspiring sight. Moreover her Fulmar fighters, which had flown on to Malta when their parent ship was damaged, had refuelled and come out again. They managed to shoot six or seven Stukas into the sea and to damage others. The

Illustrious eventually arrived off Malta at 9.45 p.m. and was safely taken into harbour."

But the battle was not over. For five days the Germans contented themselves with reconnaissance raids, and during this respite repair-work was put in hand on board the *Illustrious*. Her dead were buried at sea, her wounded, some with terrible burns, conveyed to the Imtarfa hospital. Describing the scene in the Dockyard, Mrs Norman writes: "Each day, as we came in at the gate, there was some fresh scene of devastation.

"Workshops lay piled in rubble and glass. Iron girders were twisted and torn. The docks were scarred, the truck lines rent asunder.

"The war-worn ships looked battered, black and desolate. Men's faces were grey and weary with anxiety. Over all hung a cloud of black and suffocating dust, which seemed to fill the air.

"*Illustrious* lay at the entrance to our tunnel, a target by night and by day.

"Rent and tattered, her guns still barked defiance at the enemy.

"Her officers and men came in and out of the tunnel and the surgery.

"Their faces looked lined and grimy. Their lungs were half choked and their eyes bloodshot with the dust of battle and with utter weariness.

"They had lost most of their gear. They were dressed in old boiler overalls, in grey flannel trousers and sweaters—any odd garment they had managed to save from the wrecks of the cabins.

"The surgeon of the ship had done wonderful work in the battle at sea. He was pale, and his face was very, very sad.

"It was the first time I had ever been on board a wounded ship. When I saw *Illustrious*'s great torn decks, the aching chasm that reached into her bowels, the little sick-bay that had known such horror, I felt almost as near tears as when I talked with her tired seamen . . .

"It seemed impossible that *Illustrious* would put to sea again, but she was in Malta dockyard—the dockyard that just could not be defeated . . ."

The Commander (E) in charge of repairs took stock of the torn aircraft carrier and simply said: "Her engines are not too bad, we'll get her away all right."

This they did; but not before another determined attempt had been made to sink her. This occurred on the 16th January, a day still vividly remembered in Malta. Malta, as George Grech has recalled, is used to loud bangs. The detonations of the *mortali*, or petards, at fiestas is so deafening as to call forth protests from foreigners used to a lower scale of decibels: Maltese children simply sleep through it. But never in all its days had Malta heard such pandemonium as broke out on that sixteenth of January. "That day", writes Mrs Norman, "came the first really heavy bombing raid we had experienced. Wave after wave of Junkers 88's and 87 dive-bombers swept in over the dockyard. None could deny the courage of the first German pilots to tackle our defences. They seemed to swoop within a few hundred feet of the target, diving almost vertically through a hail of flak [anti-aircraft fire]."

The Royal Malta Artillery unit on the Barracca, high above the Grand Harbour tore their A.A. guns from their moorings (so an eye-witness has told me) and tipped them downwards, so as to aim at, and hit, the Stukas flying *below* them.

"The dockyard and the harbour were a living hell beneath the low-hung curtain of the first mighty air battle. The rest of the Island became as a grandstand around the wild arena. Ye Gods! What a reception we gave the intruders! How our defences had grown since the first day of war six months ago! Every gun in the fortress blazed defiance. The air was rent with wild crescendo. Bombs screamed down. Splinters and machine-gun bullets pattered in the streets like rain. Heedless of the overwhelming odds, heedless of the deadly cloud of our own barrage, the Hurricane fighters streaked into the vortex. On roof-tops the people shouted, cheered, gasped . . . And in the mind of all was the thought—'Now we have faced the Germans too. We can take it—we can hit back—we are proud!' "

Many people died that day. Some of them were attackers, others Maltese civilians. Senglea had been pulverised, and a general flight from the ruins took place. Not a few sought refuge in the 'popular rendezvous' of the Floriana railway tunnel. Among them was the citizen who not long ago kindly unlocked for me the door which now closes it. It is an eerie place to be in. There it lies, dark and ragged, at a double remove from the life of today fifty feet above. You go down first of all to the old railway station itself, you walk along the platform, past the old lamp-standard. You see the passengers of fifty years ago, in their straw-hats and their stiff collars. They are going home after the day's work to their cosy and comfortable homes in Hamrun, in Attard, in Rabat, "rich men, furnished with ability living peaceably in their habitations." They fade from before your eyes as you enter the tunnel itself. There, above the uneven floor (for today the tunnel houses telephone cables laid below what used to be the permanent way), you see the remains of the bunks that gave rest to the crowded sleepers, in three tiers, some of them supported on wooden frames, others on stanchions driven into the yielding rock, now twisted and rusty relics of bygone distress. Every so often there is a baffle-wall, with a smaller wall behind its narrow door, as a precaution against blast. Here it was that the orphans of the storm found shelter—shelter and hope and confidence.

The *Illustrious*, wonderful to relate, had been hit only once during this day of havoc, and suffered only minor damage. But a holocaust was only narrowly averted. The merchantmen *Essex* was carrying 4,000 tons of ammunition. A bomb landed fair and square in her engine-room. Had that bomb been deflected by only a few yards, the resulting explosion must have wrecked not only the dockyard and the remains of Senglea, but Valetta as well. The ship's crew aided by volunteers managed to quell the flames just before they reached the explosives.

On the 17th reconnaissance planes came over to take stock of the position. It must have been discouraging, to say the least, to the Germans to find that despite their daring, and the heavy losses they had suffered, both the *Illustrious* and the *Essex* were still afloat. On the 18th, the airfields were the target, four of the raiders being shot down. On the 19th yet another raid was launched against the indestructible ship. A bomb which exploded on the bottom of the dock did some damage, the upward blast having the effect that an exploding mine would have. Would she ever leave Malta? It seems almost unbelievable that she did. The damage to her hull was made good and on the night of the 23rd, she slipped out to sea, and making 24 knots reached Alexandria two days later "cheered to the echo by the *Warspite* and other ships as she steamed slowly past." "That *Illustrious* episode stands out", says Cunningham, "as a triumph for British ship-building and our Naval Constructors, as well as for those who repaired her at Malta. I sent a message to the Vice-Admiral at Malta expressing our warmest appreciation of the work done under conditions of great difficulty to get the ship away. The men of Malta dockyard deserved all the praise we could give them."

The War Cabinet sent a message of thanks to General Dobbie, who in his reply said, "By God's help, Malta will not weaken." On the same day, the 20th, the Governor broadcast to the people of Malta his own appreciation of their splendid behaviour. "All will be well," he ended, "so put your trust in God and carry on." The people of Malta did both.

The Lords of the Admiralty were equally appreciative. In reply, Vice-Admiral Sir Wilbraham Ford said: "The Dockyard is continuing, and will continue to carry on giving their best work. Let them All Come!"

The *Illustrious* made her way to Norfolk, Virginia, where she was completely reconditioned.

It had been a famous victory. The convoy had arrived, the goods had been delivered; but the cost in warships had been prohibitive. Britain's few carriers could not be risked in so hazardous way again. This meant that in future, Malta itself must take their place, and become the nerve centre and the muscle of the battle. At the time neither side fully understood the ultimate implications of this thesis. With the exception of Field-Marshal Rommel the Germans, although they had entered the Mediterranean convinced that the neutralisation of Malta must have first priority, never did, and even Rommel disregarded it at a crucial juncture with fatal results for the Axis.

More than twelve years later, the captain of the *Illustrious*, the late

Admiral Sir Denis Boyd, recalled in a broadcast what he called "some of the fun, the nobility and the charm of a period and of a ship." After 'working up' in the Caribbean, this new aircraft-carrier, the first of her kind, set out in July 1940 "to assist the Mediterranean Fleet in their task of holding the eastern end of that sea. In August we met them off Malta and promptly started a fantastic life under Admiral Andrew Cunningham . . . Life from that day until the end was fairly exciting. We escorted a convoy to Malta on the average every month, depending on the moon. We had to fly off and on within the area of the Fleet by day, because of the submarine menace; but at night we were sent off with an escort to do what we could by bombing the Italian bases–Rhodes, Leros, Benghazi, Taranto and others. Then by daylight we would return to the slow moving convoy and up would go the fighters as an umbrella and out would go the Swordfish. Of course we were attacked again and again, but so efficient were the pilots of our inefficient aircraft and our radar that not a bomb hit any ships while the *Illustrious* was there, and we took heavy toll of enemy aircraft. I don't think you can realise how thin was our red line. During these months of battle we could never put more than four fighters in the air at a time. We had only sixteen, and only ten spare engines . . . Yet we were absurdly, unreasonably happy . . .

"Of course Taranto got a lot of publicity and was indeed a good show. We couldn't get the Italians into a position where they would have to fight. So Admiral Lyster and his staff designed an attack on the strongly fortified port of Taranto. Having taken a convoy to Malta, the Fleet moved into a covering position while *Illustrious* flew off the attacking aircraft as soon as it was dark from near the island of Cephalonia on the Greek coast. Only nineteen Swordfish took part; nine were to dive-bomb selected points and attract attention from the very vulnerable torpedo-carrying aircraft. It all worked like a charm. Three Italian battleships found themselves sitting on the bottom of the main harbour, and the dive-bombers damaged two cruisers and some oil tanks. Meanwhile we anxiously awaited their return and seventeen came back, to our great surprise, I must say." The pilots had little to say when they got back. "There wasn't much to say. I had sent them to sink the Italian Fleet: they had, and all they now wanted was eggs and bacon.

"... That ended our personal war with Italy. From now on we were up against the Germans, who sent some five hundred aircraft down to Sicily. This was awkward, as we had to shepherd a convoy from the West. On 11th January, a lovely day, off Pantelleria we were first attacked by torpedo aircraft. These were not much of a menace, but then came a series of brilliant dive-bombing attacks. Near misses on all sides were followed by three hits, one right through the flight deck, exploding in the hangar and setting fire to all the aircraft in it." This bomb killed all but one of those who were in the hangar. "But this I did not know at the time. All I knew was that this great ship and all we had put into her was in a bad way. The whole hangar was ablaze. Our steering gear had gone, we were going round in a circle, and the convoy and the Fleet went on, as, of course, they had to. Five more attacks came in before we got to Malta eight hours later, steering on our engines, and we were hit by three more bombs. Half our guns were out of action, the whole of the afterpart being in a fearful mess, but Acworth kept the undamaged guns firing, or we would never have survived ... I wrote at the time 'If it had not been for the blind obedience of everyone on board we would never have got into Harbour.'

"During all our battles the Padre stood near me on the bridge, broadcasting to the whole ship what was going on. His calm voice not only steadied the nerves, but let everyone live his part more fully. One stoker wrote to his wife, 'I have never seen anything like it. He was fifty feet below deck all the time, yet in a sense he had seen it.'

"Getting into Harbour was tricky ... Tired and incidentally very hungry as our cooks had been killed and the galley damaged, I went down at last to see what had happened to our beloved ship and to see the wounded. Among them was a young officer who was obviously dying. I sat by him just to see him on his way, when suddenly he tried to speak. I bent down to listen and all he wanted to say was, 'Glad you got the old ship in safely', and having made this final dedication of selfless thought, he happily died."

7

FALSE DAWN

1941

The year 1941 seemed to have opened auspiciously for Malta. True, the *Luftwaffe* had introduced a new rigour into the air attack. On that first day fifty-three civilians had been killed, largely because the populace had become almost indifferent to the activities of the Italian Air Force. But very soon they learned to take cover and the casualty rate fell rapidly. The *Luftwaffe* inspired awe, rather than terror, and in some cases respect as well. A Gozo friend of mine has described how a German plane spotted the ferry which plies between Malta and Gozo. It was crowded with passengers. The German pilot shadowed it until it reached the Gozo port, and the passengers had disembarked. He then swooped low, and waved his arm away from the ship, to indicate that no-one should go near it. When everyone was safely out of range, he sank the empty ship. No-one was hurt. The Island's defences, apart from the ground barrage, were almost negligible. At one time six Hurricanes were its only air protection. There might be three Fulmars from the *Illustrious* and perhaps one of the famous Gladiators. Sixteen Axis planes were shot down, but still the awful raids continued, all during January, February and March.

In Mrs Lee's words, "There was no feeling of contempt for the German squadrons when they arrived in Sicily. That was when the struggle for existence began—not at first in the food sense—but in the problem of finding the time to eat. The Germans kept up a steady timetable of raids—dawn—midday—dusk and an occasional extra thrown in. When the day's work and meals both had to be fitted in, these raids didn't leave much time to spare, but we've all discovered that bombs go down better when one is well fed. So we got up at dawn, and made sure of our breakfast before they came. By now we began to learn that two and more bombs can and do fall in the same place, and most people began to seek shelters under sixty feet of rock. Many of the bigger ones had private cubicles. While the evening raid was going on, the mother and family would sit in the main shelter, while father chipped and chipped until a small alcove was cut out. Then mother and family moved into this and a shrine was placed in a niche. From that time, the family continued underground during the raids, whatever had been interrupted above ground. Mother brought vegetables to prepare, mending, while father continued to chip and chip.

"Finally a comfortable room was ready and a few necessaries were brought in. When night raids came in addition to daytime raids these underground homes were almost permanent dwellings. Even when paraffin was severely rationed the light at the shrine in the main shelter was kept burning by very small contributions from each family. Not everybody had these cubicles—much depended on types of rock and the numbers accommodated. As more and more homes were destroyed, hundreds of people had to live permanently in a hole in the rock. Only dire necessity forced us to use the shelters. Attacks were too exciting to miss. We groaned when our Hurricanes couldn't overtake the Messerschmidt 109; we cheered ourselves hoarse when gunners or fighters found their target, and blazing machines hurtled to earth followed by swaying parachutists.

"One of my most vivid memories is of an attack by about fifty dive-bombers on a non-military evacuation camp. It was the third attack of the day and most of the families had gone to the more adequate shelter after the first surprise attack—about ten of us were helping to clear the debris. Soon it was clear that a third attack was coming. We split up into twos. My husband and I lay face downward in a trench and covered our faces to prevent dust suffocation. Just as the familiar whistles and dives began, a small dog leapt into the trench, flew over the top of us and fixed himself between us and the walls of earth. I was afraid he would go mad with fright and bite us so I tried to calm him by patting him and speaking to him.

His fur was literally standing on end and as still as hedgehogs' quills. I can feel it now. But I think his fear helped me to forget my own and saved me from abject terror as about 100 to 150 high explosives rained down around us. We all came out alive, though one trench was lost in a thirty foot crater."

Just when things looked critical, a change in German plans altered the situation. Once again, it must be emphasised that the Axis High Command never did grasp the real menace of Malta. During this very period, the Royal Navy established in Malta a submarine base which was to wreak havoc on the Italian convoys bound for North Africa. "Stop all supplies from Italy to Tripoli", was Dobbie's terse order. On this front, fortune seemed to be smiling on British arms. Tobruk had fallen to Wavell's army on the 22nd January, and by the 6th February, the Italians had been driven from Cyrenaica. Hitler now made a daring move: he decided to form an Afrika Korps, and by the beginning of February it was being transported to Africa. At the same time, in order to stiffen the Italian defence, half of CAT X was transferred to North Africa. This involved painful losses to British convoys supplying the army, but it had the by-product, as it were, of relieving the pressure on Malta just when the Island's situation was becoming critical.

Let us turn again to the Italian official history. "It is interesting to record," it writes "in this connection, an appreciation made by the Italian Navy, dated the 27th January, 1941, in which with the greatest clarity is discussed the problem of the neutralisation of Malta.

"Given that in the first months of war the air attacks of a systematic character had almost completely annihilated the operation of such an enemy base in both the naval and the air fields"—thus permitting the security of traffic with Libya and the utilisation of Sicilian bases by the naval forces in a manner which made possible the surveillance of the Sicily Channel with surface craft and preventing the enemy from mine-sweeping — it became abundantly clear that Malta had resumed its aero-naval function when in the succeeding months the constant hammering was suspended; that had given place to:

"Putting out of action, or almost, of the naval bases of Sicily with the practical renunciation on our part of the control of the Sicily Channel;

"Putting out of action, or almost, of the port of Naples, compelling our naval forces to station themselves farther north, completely renouncing their strategic position and allowing the enemy to operate in Italian waters even with diminished forces;

"Repeated attacks on the harbour of Tripoli;

"Attacks on our traffic with Libya. Such attacks were shown to be most grave at this time by the planting of magnetic mines on the coastal routes of Tunisia."

Taking into account then, that the action of the CAT had blocked almost at a stroke in the first days of its attack the air activity of the enemy there became urgently clear "the necessity for resuming in full the systematic action against Malta".

And so for the rest of the winter season the ding-dong contest went on. "The Germans continued their bombardment of the Island, dropping magnetic and acoustic mines in the Grand Harbour and Marsaxlok, constantly attacking the runways of the airfields, with special effect on the 5th March, and the harbours. The raids, by day and night, caused little harm to the Maltese, but caused considerable damage in the port installations, the dockyard and Sliema", over which the retiring pilots were wont to jettison their spare bombs. Volunteers went in search of unexploded, or time-fused bombs after every raid. The coast was watched and so was the sky. The *Times of Malta* of the 15th February in an article on 'The Island's Defence' set out to convince its readers that the defensive artillery was capable of countering attacks from the sky, but dropped a hint that armed peasants might open fire on parachutists before they reached the ground, in areas where they would not be within range of the artillery or the forts. "On the whole, the defence was efficient, and the base continued to function and to be reinforced, even if the pressure maintained against it prevented it for the time being from deploying all its offensive strength. Convoys arriving from the east in February and March brought reinforcements of men and material, while fighter aircraft flew into the Island in ever-increasing numbers. Both Churchill and Cunningham always had in mind, and as a first priority, the needs of Malta, and it is undeniable that their tenacity, combined with that of the defenders of the base, constituted a discouraging factor for the attackers, who were constrained to concentrate to the bitter end on the same objectives without having any clear notion of success. Even the *Luftwaffe* dive-bombers no longer showed the same determination as they had at first."

This, the official Italian summing-up of the situation, is of great interest.

Meanwhile the Germans were making renewed efforts to break the stalemate, which, as already seen, was slowly but surely developing in favour of Malta. Admiral Raeder decided to have it out with Hitler. On the 3rd February there took place an interview at which Raeder put forward his views. He pointed out that the strategic situation in the Mediterranean had been radically altered by the advance of Wavell in Cyrenaica, and by the events on the Greco-Albanian front. This had resulted in a substantial come-back of Malta's potential; and since Hitler had decided at the Berghof in January to support the Italians in order to save a loss of prestige on the part of the Axis, the admiral pressed for the 'radical solution' of the Malta problem. The necessity of subjugating the Island was debated at the 3rd February meeting in the presence of the military chiefs of Germany.

Even at this distance of time, Hitler's decision must excite our fascinated surprise. He said that he consented to plans being drawn up for the taking of Malta, but only after the rout of Soviet Russia, which he was already preparing to attack!

This same point of view was confirmed in the directives of the 15th and 23rd February; in vain did Raeder, on the 18th, press for an immediate action, which would have to be carried out by airborne troops, before the offensive in the west. This time the Führer's objections were based on something that no-one but he could have thought of—the fact that Malta was—and is—intersected by innumerable dry-stone walls, which would prevent aircraft from landing. How many farmers or tourists realise, as they walk about the Island, and traverse its country lanes, that the stones on either side of them deflected an invasion, by the express order of Hitler himself?

Raeder's determination—fruitless as it turned out—to press his point of view must have been strengthened by the opinions expressed by those responsible for the Italian Navy to their German colleagues at a meeting at Merano on the 13th/14th February. The Italian view was set out in a memorandum, No 31 of the 10th February, which did not fail to make the point, in connection with the bases used by the fleet, that the "best situated base would be Augusta, but its proximity to Malta precludes its use for the greater part of our forces so long as Malta remains unneutralised."

As a matter of fact, a plan for the attack on Malta was prepared, and in Germany too, during February and March 1941. The guiding idea of the German plan—which appeared however to have been somewhat invalidated from the start by the Hitlerian preconception to put it into action only after the collapse of Russia—was that the whole operation should be undertaken by German forces. Two divisions were to be employed, one of parachutists and one of air-borne infantry, supported by specialist units and an all-out action by the *Luftwaffe*. The landing was to be from the air, after the destruction and disruption of the principal defensive works following on the bringing into action of the striking force of the air-force. CAT X was to supply the machines for attack, escort and transportation. The invasion was conceived as an air attack, and a naval landing was envisaged solely as a subsidiary operation; so that the Italian Navy would have had a secondary rôle in the action, intervening with limited numbers after the decisive thrust had been given by the German units. It seems that the plan, which had been drawn up without any previous consultation with the Italian command, was no other than the development of Raeder's idea, which as we have already seen, had been blocked by the Führer via the dry-stone walls. It may be said, however, that at a certain moment he may have thought of Rommel as the commander best fitted to realise the undertaking, given the fact that the marshal himself, in the passage in his memoirs in which he states that he had offered to conquer the fortress writes, "and I am convinced that I should have succeeded, with the contingents of troops I had requested, and with an adequate support of air and naval forces" (*War without Hate*, Italian edition, p. 227). But the men and the means were simply not there, even if the 7th German parachute division did go on intensifying its training to be launched against an objective still not specified, which could be Malta just as well as Crete.

So the bombardment of the Island continued, and 'neutralisation' started to have the same effect, or lack of it, as 'sterilisation'. Malta lived in a state of siege, but reinforcements continued to arrive and the danger to the Italian air and naval bases increased. On the 3rd April, twelve Hurricanes mark II flew in, and another twenty-three on the 27th, and then in May other strong contingents. On the 21st forty-eight were despatched, of which all but one arrived. In all, during April and May no less than 224 Hurricanes reached Malta, which meant that compared with January, the striking force of the Island had been multiplied five times. Henceforth the Italo-German attacks became ever more difficult and dangerous.

Meanwhile the battle of Matapan had been fought and won—that extraordinary engagement during which in the darkness of the night, two Italian cruisers and two destroyers were blown to bits in four minutes and a third cruiser finished off at leisure. Once again, as Cunningham generously underlined in his despatch reporting the action, it was the Fleet Air Arm who had been the harbingers of victory. In his autobiography he makes this comment: "More important still [than the destruction of the enemy ships], the supine and inactive attitude of the Italian fleet during our subsequent evacuations of Greece and Crete was directly attributable to the rough handling they had received at Matapan. Had the enemy's surface ships intervened in these operations, our already difficult task would have been well nigh impossible." Which ominous sentences prepare us, amid prospects of progress and protection so bright, prospects towards which the Royal Navy, the Royal Air Force, Wavell and his army, even stonewall Hitler himself had all contributed, to turn and contemplate the awful murk of the wrath to come.

The famous railway tunnel shelter. Left: a mason excavates a private shelter. Maltese masons still put the handkerchief to its original use of 'head-cover'.

Soldiers and citizens work together as harvesters. Below: Italian troops practising the invasion of Malta near Spezia. It was never attempted.

8

COMET AND TOTAL ECLIPSE

1941

One evening, early in 1941, I was motoring along the darkened sea-front of Aden, in order to go on board one of H.M.'s ships for dinner, when I thought I saw in the sky to my left, an unusually bright body. When I reached the landing-stage, I was able to examine it more closely. Sure enough it was a comet. Remembering Milton's reference to the influence of a comet which "with threat of change perplexes monarchs", I turned to a Somali porter standing near me, and pointing to the comet, asked him in Arabic what it meant. "Ah!" he said, "Abu Dheneb! [father of the tail]. The last time I saw him was in 1918, just before Ghalium [Wilhelm, the kaiser] fell: this one means that the Italians will be driven from my country and the emperor of Abyssinia restored."

My friend was right. Already General Cunningham, brother of the admiral, had started to move northwards on Abyssinia. (By a happy coincidence the comet was known as Cunningham's, after the American astronomer who had first identified it.) General Platt was advancing in the southern Sudan. By the 22nd January Tobruk was in British hands. On the 25th the *Illustrious* arrived at Alexandria. Surely now the motto which shines from the throne in the Hall of St Michael and St George in the Palace at Valetta was to be fulfilled—'the presage of better days to come'. Alas, it was not. "Of the several periods of the Second World War", writes Macintyre, "during which Britain's hopes of avoiding defeat seemed to have shrunk almost to vanishing point, few can have been more fraught with doom than the spring and early summer of 1941."

What had brought about this utter reversal of fortune? It is almost Greek in its tragic impact, and indeed it was from Greece that it sprang.

As a strategist, Hitler was restless rather than rational. He was already committed on one front, the North African, and as we have seen, he had already decided to undertake another campaign, this time in defiance of what Lord Montgomery has tersely described as one of the basic rules of warfare, 'Never march on Moscow'. The rational line of action would have been, it might be assumed, to press home the African attack, occupy Egypt and thus drive the English not only out of Africa but out of the war altogether.

This done, the Russian campaign could be undertaken with almost complete immunity from interference. For his failure to do this there appear to have been two interconnected reasons. The first is that in order to bolster up his reeling partner, Hitler had been compelled to intervene in the Balkans. By a chain reaction, Britain was in honour bound to come to the aid of Greece. This could only be done by a drastic weakening of Wavell's army, and the transference of thousands of his troops to Greece. This was the only honourable course, but it involved the double disaster of so weakening the African front that the Italo-German army were able to attack on the 31st March with such effect that by the 3rd April Benghazi had fallen and the British were in full retreat; and that on the 6th April, the German 12th army crossed the frontier from Bulgaria into Greece and in less than three weeks had occupied the whole country. By the 21st April, it was obvious that our troops which had been despatched there with so much toil and danger must be evacuated. In the end, thanks to the navy, and the superb discipline of the English troops (an Athenian friend of mine who was with them still recalls their behaviour with admiration and amazement) 50,732 troops, that is eighty per cent of those originally sent there, were safely taken off. It was for Crete that they made.

The battle for Crete was one of the most dramatic, spectacular and misinterpreted actions of the whole war. The fact that, with a large part of the Greek army, the Greek royal family had found a refuge there, naturally unleashed a fountain of well-publicised slush; Patrick Leigh-Fermor's kidnapping of a German general lent a Scarlet Pimpernel atmosphere to the affair—it was indeed an amazing feat of cool-headed bluff. Finally, the fact that the invasion was the first to be effected solely by airborne troops, and that it was to all appearances successful, at once gave it an aura of triumph. In fact, when we look back on it, without in any way detracting from the skill and bravery of the invaders, we find that it was the defeated defenders who ultimately benefited from the battle.

The English decision to hold Crete at all costs has often been criticised, both at the time and in later years. The decision was, no doubt, yet another example of the lack of understanding of what could and could not be done in the face of absolute air superiority. General (afterwards Field-Marshal Lord) Wilson when asked by his old friend and chief General Wavell for his opinion, and 'Jumbo Wilson' was a man of keen intelligence if ever there was one, replied, "Unless all three services are prepared to face the strain of maintaining adequate forces up to strength, the holding of the island is a dangerous commitment." Adequate air strength simply did not exist.

The German plan had been drawn up by General Kurt Student, at that time commanding *Fliegerkorps XI* (Parachute and Airborne troops) in central Germany. Hitler, with his eye on the Russian campaign, without even consulting his Army or Navy general staff, gave his consent to the proposal that the whole operation should be carried out by the *Luftwaffe* to the sole glory of the ambitious Goering. It very nearly ended in calamity.

The value of Crete to the Germans was twofold. First, it created what was to be known as 'bomb alley' that is the sea lane between Alexandria and the middle Mediterranean, both sides of which, with the British beaten back to the confines of Egypt once more, would be at the mercy of Axis bombers. Secondly, it was an important, indeed vital, stepping-stone towards the promised land of one of Hitler's most grandiose dreams. He had decided to be another Alexander, another Trajan, a second Napoleon, and to become master of the Levant and of its boundless reservoirs of oil, of which Germany was already dangerously short. To this end, he had for some time been fostering unrest in Iraq. His active and skilful minister in that country, Herr Grobba, had carried on an intensive and highly successful propaganda campaign, to which the British made no reply whatever. I once, a few years later, asked an Iraqi officer why he and his like, intelligent young patriots, had fallen for the German 'line'. "Simply because", he answered, "you never made any effort to contradict it: we not unnaturally assumed that it must be true." A rebellion was touched off in May 1941, the Prince Regent and the little King became refugees, the British community was forced into confinement in the grounds of the British and American embassies. In the end the revolt miscarried: Hitler never got his oil. The reason is to be found in Crete. A few aircraft, it is true, did reach Mosul in northern Iraq. They had flown from Crete, and had paused to refuel at Rayak in the Lebanon, at that time in the hands of the Vichy French, who proffered their malicious co-operation. They had hoped for secrecy and had sealed the frontiers with Palestine and Trans-Jordan. The telephone lines were cut. But they forgot one thing. Railways have their own telephone system, and railwaymen are railwaymen the world over. Thus, the station-master at Rayak was able to report, and did report, the arrival and departure of every single German aircraft using the airfield under his eyes to the headquarters of the Palestine railways at Haifa. The intelligence was speedily passed on, and countermeasures adopted. Without the promised German support, the Iraq rebellion was soon crushed. The legitimate rulers were restored, and within a few years Iraq became the first eastern state to declare war on the Axis, as the friend and ally of Great Britain.

It was in Crete that the origin of this failure is to be found. As explained in the last chapter, the Italian Navy had no intention of risking another mauling at the hands of Cunningham. The *Luftwaffe* therefore had to go it alone. It had at its disposal a total of 716 aircraft, bombers, dive-bombers, fighters and scouts. On the 20th May, 15,000 German troops were deposited on the island of Crete, some in gliders using the few airfields, the majority by parachute. The following day, they were joined by 3,000 more. The resistance of the Anglo-Greek forces was far more bitter than had been expected. Indeed, in the opinion of Cunningham and others, had two battalions which were held in reserve to repel a reinforcement from the sea been thrown into the battle, the outcome would have been defeat for the invaders. The seaborne assault was repulsed by the navy, but by the time the two battalions had reached the key landing-ground, it was too late. The battle was lost.

On the 27th it was decided to evacuate the island. In all, when the evacuation was completed on the 1st June, 18,000 men had been borne away. The navy had suffered cruel losses, three cruisers and six destroyers had been sunk, two battleships, the only aircraft-carrier, two cruisers and two destroyers damaged beyond hope of local repair, three cruisers and six destroyers less seriously damaged. It was an appalling score. But Cunningham and his oak-hearted men remained undaunted. At the beginning of the operation he had signalled to the fleet: "We must not let the army down." To the misgivings expressed by his staff he answered: "It takes the Navy three years to build a ship. It would take three hundred to rebuild a tradition." The Royal Navy is known as the silent service; but when its sailors speak, they speak with the tongues of men and of angels—and they have charity.

So ended the conquest of Crete; but not the results of it.

In the end the Cretan venture was to mark a turning-point in the fortunes of the Axis, a point at which they turned down. The reason for this paradoxical fact is to be found in one word—Malta. We must now go back a little, and once again we must see things as others saw them.

What the English did not know at the time was that the German losses in Crete were so severe that it was impossible even to contemplate another operation of the same kind. Contrary to English belief, the 7th Airborne Division was the only one that Germany possessed. That in itself spelt liberation for Malta. But there was more to it than that. The removal of the *Luftwaffe* from Sicily had enabled Malta greatly to increase her offensive power, both in the air, and, very damagingly, by the installation in Malta of a base for the new 'U' class submarines, smaller than preceding types, and ideally adapted for operating in the clear waters of the Mediterranean. The Italians were losing heart: they no longer regarded the German air force as the key to victory. Here is a quotation from their official archives, cited by Santoro in his book on the Italian Air Force in the Second World War, (Rome 1958): "The results obtained, it may be considered, did not correspond with the numerous means employed . . . On the harbour of Valetta the same units delivered numerous bombing-raids, dropping an impressive number of bombs, but the port still maintained that contracted scale of activity to which it had been reduced by the activities of the Second [Italian] Squadron. Also, the airfields, not withstanding the very large quantity of explosives hurled upon them, are today fully operational and are supplied with a number of bombers and fighters which may be presumed to be higher than that of five months ago. The opinion of the Germans about the defensive potential of the Island has changed, and is very different from what they expressed at the outset when they arrived in Sicily. Malta, according to the majority of the Germans, should have capitulated in a matter of days. The Germans, after having sampled the defensive capacity of Malta, have modified their opinion: many declare that Malta has become a very tough proposition, comparable only to Narvik."

J. M. A. Gweyr, in *Grand Strategy*, Vol. III, part 1, (*History of the Second World War*, 1964,) sums up the matter in a sentence: "General Freyburg (commanding in Crete) and his troops, in losing the battle of Crete, had won the more important battle of Malta."

The battle of Malta raged remorselessly and uninterruptedly. More and more homes were destroyed, more and more churches violated, more and more monuments damaged or obliterated. The Casino Maltese was gutted, half of it pounded into rubble.

One morning, the citizens of Valetta were astounded to see the Palace Square covered with seaweed. Where had it come from, what freak of bombardment could possibly have deposited it there of all places? It had in fact come from the Palace itself. A bomb had crashed through the ceiling of the State dining-room. When the Palace was constructed in the sixteenth century, its Maltese architect, as a protection against the summer heat, had interposed a layer of seaweed between the ceiling of the room and the roof, rather as nowadays an architect might employ fibre-glass. This direct hit, however, did not displace the Governor or his staff. It was only a later bomb, which although not striking the Palace itself, fell by the corner nearest the Queen Victoria memorial, and created so violent a blast as to wreck every window in the building and much else. The Governor thereupon moved out to the Bugeja Institute in Hamrun, of which he and his staff occupied the northern wing, the southern being already the Police headquarters.

The casualty list mounted. No other day, indeed no single month, would equal the fifty-six lives lost on the 16th January, when the *Luftwaffe* made its first onslaught, against the *Illustrious*. During the rest of the month only nine civilian deaths are recorded. The figures for the rest of the year are: February: 15; March: 30; April: 47; May: 28; June: 5; July: 40; August: 10; September: 1; October: 10; November: 7; December: 31; or 289 in all. The true figure may well have been higher. To these must be added military casualties. Many Maltese were serving in the armed forces, some in the Navy, the majority with the Royal Malta Artillery—as already recorded, the very first casualties in the Island had been one of their gun-crews—and the King's Own Malta Regiment. The great majority of these men were volunteers. General Dobbie had broadcast on the 4th February that preparations were being made "for the conscription of manpower for the combatant and non-combatant services". But voluntary enlistment was to continue as it had been brought to the Government's notice "that many men of different ages and callings, knowing that conscription is imminent would prefer to enlist voluntarily". One of them was my friend George Grech; but he was not allowed to as he was indispensible at the Palace. "I remember I felt kind of mad about it, but when I went home and told Carrie about it, she said 'Oh thanks to God! I prayed so much so you'll be exempted'." Such must have been the tension and anxiety in many a Maltese home.

The Island's aircraft and submarines were now on the offensive. Convoys continued to arrive. "By the middle of July", writes Cunningham, "Malta was causing us acute anxiety. Except for the limited quantities of essential stores sent in in the mine-laying submarines, no supplies had reached the Island since early in May." It was therefore planned to send in a convoy from the west, a feint being made in the east, to hoodwink the enemy into believing that the convoy was destined for Alexandria. The double operation was a complete success. One destroyer was sunk, another, a cruiser and a merchantman damaged, but six large vessels with the much needed stores arrived in Malta. Moreover, the armed merchantman *Breconshire*, the hero of many a brush with the enemy, and six large 'returned empties' immobilised for so long in Malta by the air attacks, were able to make their way back to Gibraltar protected by Force H.

The convoy arrived on the 24th, and thus gave rise to what the official Italian history calls "the unfortunate action of the night of the 26th July". The story has often been told, both by English and Italian writers, and indeed by many a Maltese citizen, for "the people of the port came out to see the sport". It was an action which called for great daring and heroism on the part of those who undertook it. Its object was to force an entry into the Grand Harbour by means of a motor torpedo boats 'M.T.B.s' and 'one-man submarines' in reality human torpedoes, and to sink the ships of the convoy as they lay at anchor. The Italians had long specialised in this form of warfare; During the first war a midget submarine had succeeded in attaching mines to the Austrian battleship *Viribus Unitis* as it lay in harbour, and sinking it. The crew included the father of the future Count Ciano, Mussolini's son-in-law and foreign minister. The great anchors of the battleship still flank the main portal of the Italian Ministry of Marine in Rome.

On this later occasion the upper echelons of the Italian command showed little enthusiasm, because they knew precisely and accurately what were the physical obstacles in addition to massed artillery and aircraft that the invaders would have to overcome, namely (a) a chain of rafts armed with spikes linked with caves, a portion of which could be opened; (b) a double chain of cylindrical buoys and nets (which had been sent from Alexandria at the end of the Ethiopian campaigns and adapted to the needs of the Grand Harbour); straddling these, was generally anchored the *Westgate*, as guard-ship; (c) another double chain of cylindrical buoys which since

September 1939 had linked the St Elmo mole with the mainland; (d) finally a chain of underwater and floating obstructions below Corradino hill, for the defence of ships anchored at the Marsa. And yet these brave men came on. The plan undoubtedly derived psychological encouragement from the employment of similar vessels in Suda Bay during the Cretan campaign. But the improvised harbour of Suda Bay and Malta, one of the strongest points on earth, were very different.

During the early part of the night Malta radar had shown that small Italian units were approaching. At once, the shore batteries, mostly Maltese-manned, were stood to. Here was the opportunity they had been waiting for for so many dull months. They seized it. As the little vessels came near land in the grey light of dawn, first a shower of tracer bullets rained upon them, to give the gunners the range. Then the searchlights were turned on, and down their beams hurtled the shells. One after another, the enemy boats exploded. Some tried to turn back, but fell victims to the waiting fighters. One of our machines was shot down, but the pilot survived. He fell into the water, and made for the nearest vessel, one of the Italian E-boats. He scrambled aboard unchallenged, to find that his shipmates were eight corpses. Only one of the attackers, Major Tesei, whose assignment it was to act as a projectile to open up a way in, succeeded in arriving at his objective. He did but little damage. Not one of the ships in the harbour was hit. Every one of the invaders, between seventeen and twenty, was destroyed. The attack was a complete, if heroic, fiasco.

Here is an eye-witness account by Miss Ella Warren M.B.E., of this memorable action.

"The convoy was in! The Admiral's signal had been 'Convoy must go through'—and it fought through! Elaine and I, ready for the night-watch, walked up and down the jetty to get a little air at sunset. We were well prepared for raids and soon enough the siren sent us scuttling to the 'underground', with a subconscious glance up at the thick battlements.

"Exactly as usual we slipped off our frocks (buttoned up the front for speed and convenience) and were soon in our canvas bunks, rolled in a blanket well beneath the rock, and too tired to listen for any bumps or crumps. 'Shaken' just before midnight four of us went on duty in the cave which is our 'office'.

"Was it my fancy or was there a specially excited gleam on Mr Bowie's glasses?—sure enough he gave us the dope—slowly, in broadest Scottish, 'There's been a bit of excitement, maybe it's all over—but we were rather expecting a bom*barrd*ment, as there's something outside. You leddies are to keep this side of the rock. I'm going to bed.'

"Duly thrilled, we got down to work and nothing happened except Mr Carnes bursting in with ruffled hair and dressing-gown at 3., but it was only another raid. I fancied afterwards the raids were a blind. Several more officers in brighter coloured dressing-gowns and slightly less ruffled hair came in, and tea was brewed for at least eleven! Just before 4., it was very quiet. The watch changed and back we went to 'plotters' and slept, thinking it all a false alarm —but when we woke we heard the story.

"Now at 5. there was a sudden great commotion. The 'something outside' had loosed at dawn a couple of dozen E boats and 'mystery' boats—with a dart and a dash at the harbour entrance!

"Woken by the din, throngs of people ran along the front, puzzled at the criss-cross fire and the low searchlights just after an 'all clear'. How they cheered the guns, as they crowded on to the Barraccas! K. saw it from home and couldn't make out what was occurring, tracers, lights and noise giving the effect of a firework display!

"As the E-boats swept in they were lit up by the faint dawn; they raced through low mist, coloured by the rising sun. The guns of the harbour forts snapped and cracked. There was one explosion. An E-boat blew up against the defences. Three minutes from the start—and it was over! Like another mad charge of the light brigade—and only derelict boats remained.

"Then the Air Force took on, and further out they sunk all the rest of the approaching craft—all but one. A pilot had to bale out from a damaged aircraft, well out to sea. He swam to the drifting boat and somehow clambered on board. There was wine and blood and food and six dead men. As the light strengthened he rigged a white flag, and thus it was the only unsunk E-boat was captured by a British trawler!

"Over—and in three minutes; but thereby hangs a tale! A retired colonel, visiting his naval son, had somehow, (through his willingness to do 'anything') become the efficient commander of the harbour forts, and for two years had not ceased to train raw Maltese country lads, till they had become first-class gunners. And it was the gunnery of the sons of Malta that repelled the mad attack!

"I have stayed in this old fort, (sleeping in the Grand-Masters' store-house.) I have talked to these Maltese soldiers, perched on the outer point, with one of the constant watchers by me, and been shown the spot where they 'got' the Italians. There is nothing to see now. The quiet sea bears no trace—and the defences held and were not pierced.

"An eager group of 'us girls' were on the jetty to see Commander Dane bring in his prize. The Maltese sailors were definitely bloodthirsty over the task of burying dead Italians!

"Among things salved from the boat was a little mascot white furry dog, with a red bow; What girl gave it to her boy? We named him 'Bruno-Bianco'; he swung on a cord above my typewriter and his little black eyes gave nothing away."

According to a French authority, Drevon, writing in *Revue de Defense National* in 1954, the combined action of the naval and air forces based on Malta resulted in increasing losses to Axis shipping during the second half of 1941. He gives the following table:

Month	Tonnage Available	Tonnage sunk or damaged	%
June	118,000	8,500	7
July	153,000	27,000	17
August	156,000	39,000	25
September	163,000	63,000	40
October	50,000	32,000	63
November	37,000	28,000	77

No wonder Rommel was depressed. As he was to write not without melancholy in the last chapter of his memoirs—a pathetic chapter entitled 'Darkness surrounded us'—"If only the task were to attack and take Malta". In vain did he state his point of view in the spring of 1941. "A year later," comments the Italian history, "in the intoxicating enthusiasm created by his victory at Tobruk, even this point of view was changed."

Three other events had occurred to improve the fortunes of England and Malta. Churchill and Roosevelt had signed the Atlantic Charter aboard a British battleship in the western Atlantic. Then had come Hitler's invasion of Russia, which meant his temporary abandonment of any thought of attacking Malta. On the 21st June he wrote to Mussolini: "I have been induced to make the gravest decision of my life. The situation:—England has lost the war . . . Now my general ideas are these: . . . as regards your colonies, Duce, not even North Africa will probably be in any danger until the autumn . . . Before autumn, an attack on Egypt is out of the question." Finally on the 7th December, the massacre at Pearl Harbour, disaster though it was, brought America into the war and so guaranteed ultimate victory for the United Nations.

And yet, before the end of 1941 this brightening day was to end in utter darkness.

ACT THREE

9

INTERLUDE–ONE BOY'S WAR

1941–1942

The third act of the drama of Malta's war is an amalgam of Aeschylus and Hollywood, of inevitable horror and improbable 'cliffhangers'. In between comes an interlude, a war fought by one English boy of nineteen. It lasted five months. The story is told by the boy himself in a series of diaries. In their simple patriotism, in their unselfconscious pathos, they echo Siegfried Sassoon with undertones of A. E. Housman.

Oliver Ormrod was born on Easter Day, 16th April, 1922. He was educated at Wellington, and grew up as what was still then a typical English gentleman. He loved hunting, beagling, fencing. He loved England, too, and honour and loyalty. By the age of nineteen he was a Pilot Officer in the Royal Air Force. Many thought him to be two years younger: he was nicknamed Sonny. On the 12th November, 1941, Oliver was one of a group of pilots who flew Hurricanes off the *Argus* and landed them at Malta.

This was one of many such operations, which had been initiated and sustained by the personal interest of Churchill himself. From the very outbreak of the war, Churchill had realised (as others had not) the vital importance of the Island. Soon after the fall of France he had written: "Africa was the only continent in which we could meet our foes on land. The defence of Egypt and Malta were duties compulsive upon us, and the destruction of the Italian empire the first prize we could gain." Churchill's history of the Second World War shares two qualities with Gibbon's *Decline and Fall of the Roman Empire*. Both works are classics, and nobody reads either more than once. It may therefore be helpful in achieving some perspective of the Malta picture to quote from Churchill.

"From the beginning of January [1941] I had apprehended the arrival of the German air power in Sicily with the consequent menace to Malta and to all our hopes of resuming traffic through the Mediterranean . . . I deeply regretted that I was never able to achieve my conception of a squadron of very heavily deck-armoured ships of no more than fifteen knots bristling with A.A. [Anti-Aircraft] guns and capable of withstanding to a degree not enjoyed by any other vessel afloat both air and underwater attack. When in 1941 and 1942 the defence and succouring of Malta became so vital . . . it was then too late."

Churchill knew that with Malta totally unprovided with A.A. defence, there was every good reason for the Fleet to quit the Island. As already related, this was apparent three years earlier, during the Abyssinian crisis. But nothing had been done. Malta, Churchill noted, at the outbreak of the war, with almost negligible air defences presented "a problem for which there was no immediate solution". Churchill later admitted that he—and remember he had been out of office for almost a decade—"did not sufficiently measure the danger to, or the consequent deterrent upon, British warships from air attack." But then, who did? In June 1940, Churchill records, the Admiralty actually contemplated the abandonment of the Eastern Mediterranean, and to use Gibraltar as the main concentration base. Churchill naturally resisted this, which "seemed to spell the doom of Malta." Malta was continually in his thoughts. In September 1940, "I had a fear for Malta which seemed almost defenceless . . ." The beaches were defended on an average front of one battalion for fifteen miles. There were no reserves for counter-attack, which left the Island at the mercy of a landing-force. The danger was extreme. "We found means to reinforce Malta before any serious attack from the air was made upon it, and no one dared to try a landing upon the island fortress at any time." But the anxiety gnawed. In October 1940, "I feared greatly for Malta." On the 13th of that month Churchill wrote the following minute:

"First in urgency is the reinforcement of Malta:

(a) by further Hurricane aircraft, flown there as can best be managed;

(b) by convoy now being prepared, which should carry the largest A.A. outfit possible, as well as the battalions and the battery—I understand another M.T. ship can be made available;

(c) by one or better still two more battalions released from Police duty on the Canal or in Palestine, and carried to Malta when next the Fleet moves thither from Alexandria. General Dobbie's latest appreciation bears out the grievous need of strengthening the garrison. Every effort should be made to meet his needs, observing that once Malta becomes a thorn in the Italian side the enemy's force may be turned upon it. The movement of these reinforcements should therefore precede any marked activity from Malta.

(d) Even three Infantry tanks at Malta would be important, not only in actual defence, but as a deterrent if it were known that they were there. Some mock-up tanks might also be exhibited where they would be detected from the air."

On this remarkable prescient document two comments may be made. The first is that Dobbie, whom Churchill described as "a soldier who in fighting leadership and religious zeal recalled memories of General Gordon, and, looking farther back, of the Ironsides and Covenanters of the past", had from the outset made the practical point that it would be damaging folly to use Malta as an offensive base while her defences were so negligible, and that Churchill had adopted Dobbie's view. Secondly what happened to the tanks is not ascertainable; but a Gozo friend has assured me that three tanks did turn up in Gozo, of all places. Where should they be stationed? It was decided in the end to put them at the main cross-roads in the capital, so that they could be directed against any marauder from whichever direction he would be so foolhardy as to attempt to molest the Gozitans—a decision worthy of Ulysses, who spent several years in the Island as the guest of Calypso.

Churchill's preoccupation with Malta never wavered. He 'dreaded' the appearance of the Germans in this theatre. It was Churchill himself who suggested sending the *Illustrious* to Malta. In the summer of 1940 the first twelve Hurricanes were flown into the Island from the *Argus*, to be followed by many more. On the 31st October Suda Bay, in Crete, at the invitation of the Greeks, became a British base. This gave us a great air advantage, and the Prime Minister felt 'easier about Malta'. Throughout 1941 more and more aircraft reached the Island. Already by June no less than 224 Hurricanes and other types had landed in the fortress, all flown from aircraft-carriers, escorted by Admiral Somerville's Force H based on Gibraltar. Supplies were convoyed from the east. Churchill was able to comment: "By June, the first fierce onslaught had been repulsed, and by the skin of its teeth the island survived. Its main ordeal was reserved for 1942."

This was the Malta on which landed Oliver Ormrod on Wednesday, 12th November, 1941. "At about 2.45 or 3 o'clock we came at last out of bad visibility over Gozo. Landed at Hal Far, in Malta . . . This Island is odd. It protrudes abruptly out of the sea: yet no point on the Island rises to any great height. It is like a uniformly even piece of rock at a distance from the air. Four of us share a large comfortable ante-room. It is square, so each has a corner – P/O Allen, P/O Lowe, self and P/O McKay, reading from left to right as one enters. This is in a building called Hal Far House. Maltese architecture is rather pleasing. The Maltese seem very good mannered. The climate now is quite good. Obviously it's too hot in summer. The stone buildings seems to resist air raids well, for it just chips bits off instead of the whole building collapsing."

Such were Oliver's first impressions. Two days later, on Friday, 14th November, he makes his first journey to Valetta. "Went to Valetta in a petrol lorry about 11.30 a.m. Was very entertained by what I saw on my way to Valetta. The petrol lorry was very antique and the driver persisted in sounding his horn at frequent intervals for little or no apparent reason. The town seemed full of happy little children – some little girls with long dark hair like Maureen – and goats, which amused me by disappearing through the front doors of houses or standing haughtily on the pavements. The point that most attracted my attention was the number of pony carts and the excellence of the majority of the ponies. I saw many beautiful ponies of about fourteen hands, pulling peasants' carts, ponies that in England would be prized. They were of Arab blood, I presume. There were also many donkeys and mule-carts." In war-stricken Malta, Oliver is still the young English country lad. He joins the Union Club. He is then shown round the city. "Saw the harbours and the dwellings cut in the rock—peculiar mode of living, but useful in war-time—and went through a tunnel in the rock below the Army H.Q." Evidently there was a lull in hostilities, because Oliver and several of his brother officers spent the evening in Valetta, and stayed for the night at the Osborne Hotel in South Street. "Noble had told Potter to get me tight, but they did not succeed. Heard today that the *Ark Royal* had been torpedoed on her way back to Gibraltar. This was no doubt the unfortunate result of a day's delay at sea, waiting for suitable weather for our flight here."

Monday, 17th November, 1941

"Went down to my machine. Ran it up and tested the magnetos . . . I walked off for some exercise to Boogie Woogie—or whatever they call the town, perhaps it's Kalafrana, one or the other anyway. Wandered on along the Valetta road, hoping I might find a riding horse for hire." Oliver did manage to find a mount on several occasions. And as so many English soldiers have done before and since, he gave his own name to the town of Birzebuggia—the well of olive oil, it means in Maltese. Marlborough's warriors called *Bois le Duc*, '*Boil-Duck*', and their successors who had recently occupied Asmara at once dubbed the smart military club there—'the Croce del Sud' (since it is from that town that the Southern Cross is first descried) —the 'Soapy Crutch'. Oliver followed the same tradition.

Tuesday, 18th November, 1941

". . . Tried to get hold of a horse out of the many carts to ride to Rabat; but the natives did not seem to understand what I wanted . . . Rode on the box seat of a garry to Rabat aerodrome, driving much of the way myself. Rather amazed some airmen when I reined up beside them to ask them the whereabouts of the Officers'

Mess! . . . Found the Mess was some way off in the town on the hill overlooking the aerodrome. Started to walk but some Maltese fellows with a lorry insisted upon my taking a lift, and they took me close to the Mess in the beautiful old city of Medina . . . The Mess is in the beautiful old house of Baron Chappelle, who is away."

That same house is the very one in which I write. It is now an hotel, in which I have occupied the same room on the old ramparts during part of every winter for the past twelve years. The old aerodrome is still there, now a sward where sheep may safely graze, with the old runway used as an amateur speed-track. These very walls echoed to the laughter of this happy young warrior, and the tranquil sky before my window was the scene of battle, murder and sudden death. Generally, the pilots went down to the airfield, Ta Qali, on foot or in 'garries'; but I have been told that sometimes, like their contemporaries at universities, they found knotted sheets lowered over the ancient ramparts a quicker form of transport.

"Medina and Rabat seem to possess even more orders, more priests and more friars than Valetta. Was most amused on my way to Rabat aerodrome this afternoon by the sight of a darling little donkey drawing a cart driven by a Maltese at full gallop." Could he but come back, he would still behold the same sight. It is somehow such little notes as these rather than the battle-pieces, that link that vanished lad with the enduring world.

As Mr Galea's invaluable statistics show, the air-attacks on Malta had temporarily slackened. For the whole month of November, he records only seven civilian casualties. Things were soon to change.

Wednesday, 19th November, 1941

". . . Throughout the night the Italians launched bombers against us—on account of a convoy of ships newly arrived. Saw one a/c held beautifully by the searchlights; but the anti-aircraft just couldn't hit it. Think it would have been a beautiful target for a night-fighter, but there seemed none about—goodness knows why not, it was a very clear night . . . Was awoken once in the night by a bursting bomb."

He adds with poignant irrelevancy: "A point of interest is that of the Pacifist group that once flourished at (Wellington) the majority have been killed in action."

Friday, 21st November, 1941

"We arose to the sound of much noise. The Italians were indulging in a low flying attack on this aerodrome at 7.15 a.m. We went out to view the fun and were much pleased by the magnificent spectacle of the 'flaming onions' fired by the Beofords [*sic*] guns. Saw one stream of 'onions' pass through a 'vie' of three Maccies.

"When the ack-ack had died down we witnessed a 'dog fight' between seven of 185 squadron and some Maccies. Apparently the 185 boys had 'jumped' some of the enemy and then been 'jumped' in turn by more of the Italians. The Maccies powered by Daimlers-Benz (German) engines are superior to our Hurricanes in performance.

"It was most infuriating to see such a fight and we not in it. A fortune teller told me I would survive this war, but if my survival is brought about by the misfortune to miss all action, then I am indeed a most unfortunate individual. It would be better to die in action. To survive this war without ever having been in action is most shameful for a fighter pilot."

The days went by. Looking after the aircraft and their armament by day, going down to bathe—it must have been an exceptionally warm year—in the afternoon, taking care not to be caught by the trip-wires affixed to the shore defence mines, reading—and becoming rather bored.

Tuesday, 25th November, 1941

". . . Started the afternoon in a very ill humour. Might as well be still a civilian for all the action I've seen. How miserable I feel when I read in the papers of fierce battles elsewhere. Thought of going to Marsa and riding that grey, but it looked like rain, so I didn't . . . If I wet this uniform I have no other to wear instead. Besides there is nowhere much to ride."

Monday, 1st December, 1941

"But for this diary me-thinks I'd lose all sense of time, only this keeping me in mind of daily dates. Are we never to move? Never to operate? Never to fight? Miss everything?"

Friday, 5th December, 1941

". . . I spent the day in hatred of all men, so fed up with being here doing nothing."

Saturday, 6th December, 1941

"Spent most of the day reading more about Alexander [the Great: Oliver was a great reader of military biography.] I had thought of going to Valetta in the afternoon, but feeling insatiable decided that it was no good going. I was in this mood because I long for operations. Absolutely long to experience the object of my training—battle."

This eager boredom continued into the next months. Oliver was not happy. He was distressed by the laxity of discipline in certain quarters, the 'deboucheries' as he calls them in Valetta made no appeal to him, and he was deeply disturbed to discover that one of his brother-officers was a coward. Such circumstances are part of the undertones of war; but to a reader of twenty-five years later the really appalling feature of this situation is the inefficiency of the Station. There were still no proper dispersal-pens, or, as Oliver thought more useful and easily constructed in the soft Malta rock, underground hangars, and the aircraft could only be manœuvred on to the runway with the greatest difficulty. On Tuesday, 9th December, Oliver writes: "We are to do the manual work of unbogging aircraft where they have sunk in the muddy dispersals ourselves . . . We went round the dispersals in a gang. We pushed, pulled and lifted aircraft out of the mud and turned all aircraft so that they are ready to be taxied straight out when required . . . Hope we may get a spell of dry weather to facilitate the work." And on the following day: "Up a little earlier than usual. Attempted to move my aircraft but it got bogged . . . After luncheon I got my aircraft over the mud on to the taxi track by means of tracks of corrugated iron sheets. Collected some airmen to push for fear that if I used the engine, the ends of some of the sheets of corrugated iron might be prised up and hit the propeller."

This half schoolboy, half grown-up life, with descriptions of parties in the mess, and oddities of behaviour, was soon cut short.

Friday, 19th December, 1941

"Enemy aircraft are busy all today, because a convoy has just docked in the Grand Harbour." And on the following day: "There have been various air raids lately in honour of the convoy in Valetta harbours. This morning, just after breakfast, out of a sky spread with clouds an attack was made. We had been warned that a plot of fifty was on board, so we were up on the roof to see the fun. (Wish we'd been up in the air but we are not here for that.) Soon the barrage was in full blast. An 88 dived down from the sun and we saw its bomb, falling from it (at about six or seven thousand feet I suppose). Then it went off through the thick of the barrage. Some bursts were very close but it kept on going and passed out of sight. Only saw this one 88, but after a lull of a quarter of an hour, three more attacked . . . 249 squadron destroyed an 88 and a 109, possibly another 88 too, but lost an odd Hurricane or two being jumped by the escorting fighters, Maccies and ME 109's that formed the majority of the plot. (This was all out of our sight.) Anyway it shows that the Huns have returned from Rusher [*sic*] and mean to spend a happy winter in the Mediterranean. Not too good for the Hurricane boys here, 109's having a much superior performance to old Hurricanes, which under the circumstances, as experienced in the Battle of Britain etc, have always had a 'high cover' of Spitfires to deal with enemy fighters, whilst they dealt with bombers. There are no Spitfires here, nor is there any time to gain much height after the warning has been given before the enemy arrives—what are wanted here are the fast aircraft like Whirlwinds, because the disadvantage of their comparatively low ceiling does not matter when it be remembered that defending aircraft have not time to gain much height before the enemy arrives anyway.

"Took my varey pistol out of my machine to have it cleaned. If only they'd built underground hangars in peacetime. It would have made no end of a difference and here they could be constructed more easily than anywhere else. Everything weathers and rusts at dispersals. Energy is wasted replacing parts that have thus been rendered unserviceable without flying. Time is wasted moving from aircraft to aircraft. Petrol is wasted transporting material to the dispersals. N.C.O's cannot properly supervise men, so spread out, aircraft are damaged taxiing. Aircraft get stuck in the mud. It takes time to bring out an aircraft to fly on the aerodrome. Ground straffing enemy aircraft could do great damage. A lot of valuable land is covered by the dispersals. As opposed to this, though, to build underground hangars is obviously not a simple matter, yet here it is made easier by the rock that can be so easily tunnelled as witnessed by the catacombs, air-raid shelters etc. Admittedly, fittings for air ventilation would have to be fitted, but that could surely be done as in underground railways etc? I'm told that such hangars were not constructed because it was erroneously supposed the Maltese would be pro-Italian and we would lose the Islands."

"Old, unhappy, far off things, and battles long ago?" Perhaps, but to read in Malta this remarkable summary of the situation, as it was in Malta in December 1941, written by a nineteen-year-old boy, is to feel something at least of the pity, if not the terror, which Aristotle prescribed as being the elements of true tragedy.

Yes, the Germans were back, and day after day Oliver minutely describes their raids, on Valetta, the Harbour, and on the aerodromes. But Oliver was still a mere spectator. On Christmas Eve he writes: ". . . Suppose we are to do nothing. I am very vexed. This business is shaming our honour. Might just as well be civilians for all we do. I am ashamed when I find us mere spectators of 'dog-fights'. If only we would move off on the operation that brought us here without delay, or become operational here for a time until the time for our move comes." It is to be inferred from earlier references in the diary that Oliver thought that his squadron was destined for the North African campaign.

Not all his brother-officers were so irked by inaction. ". . . Though they agree that they wish they were 'up there', when I call their attention to our disgraceful position, they do not seem to worry unduly. It is the fact they are here at all and without much luggage that annoys them, and I heard them declare how glad they would be if the war were to end today; for my part nothing would horrify me more than that it should end before I have a chance to satisfy my honour for my country and my family; indeed the thought of such a thing terrifies me.

"Little did I think that on becoming an operational pilot I should spend seven months inactive. I am deeply agitated and ashamed." On Christmas evening there was as might be expected much gaiety in the Mess. "I read until about 10.30 p.m. by which time the drinks had gone round to some effect. Then talking to my C.O. about what was to be our chances of operating. Some others asked him where it had been intended we should, this he said he might not tell them, although the operation was cancelled. However, after the others had moved off, he told me the original plan so long as I made no mention of it. (I shall leave a blank, so that at the end of some *lapse of time* I may record it. It is interesting. What Potter told me fits in. This is more definite than that.) This illustrates the danger of alcohol causing officers to give away secrets, which they should not, though of course it was just what I was hoping to find out definitely."

For the remaining few days of the year the raids continued. Not all the raiders escaped. On Sunday the 28th December, Oliver records: "A soldier took me to see one of the corpses lying by the side of the road. The poor devils had been disintegrated, a description here would avail no useful purpose. I was shocked by a Maltese workman dancing round a stray leg shouting: 'The——, I piss on his leg tomorrow morning!' Those airmen died nobly for their country and their Führer; even though they be our enemies, whatever their crimes, that fact we should acknowledge. They were military airmen whatever else." Yet a little later on the same day he can add—"When I returned to the Mess X said jokingly 'Did you smell cooking German', and was hardly ready for my answer: 'Yes! —I had'. Personally the corpses moved me but little more than a bird I might have shot down. After all, why should they? They are fundamentally the same. It is weakness of nerves that sees more to it than that."

Tuesday, 30th December, 1941

"According to the *Times of Malta* there have been sixty air raids in the past week. The *Times of Malta* publishes a very one-sided account of the air operations over this Island. German losses sound quite impressive when our losses are not mentioned. As for the bombing of Luqa, that has been dismissed as 'slight damage to Government property'." This paragraph is worth recording, not as the slightest criticism of the *Times of Malta*, which—as already recorded—continued publication on every single day throughout the war, sometimes appearing with its edges singed by incendiary bombs, but as witness to the alertness of the Island censorship to the enemy's intelligence network, which, however contrived, remained remarkably efficient.

The previous day, Oliver had attained his heart's desire: he had flown in combat. Not with his own squadron, but attached to No. 242. His account of the ensuing 'dog-fight' is enthralling, but so technical as to be almost unintelligible except as a sort of incantation. "We were on the point of attacking, but down came the Messerschmidts before we could. I saw them, little silver specks above us (I had not seen the Junkers as I had to concentrate on joining formation for attack.) "Duck" was shouted [i.e. half the formation turn steep to port the other half steeply to starboard] Hurricanes passing at all angles, think 109's had come and gone by now . . . The mêlée dispersed. I was over Hal Far at seven or eight thousand feet . . . The radio telephone was telling someone to land. I couldn't make out who. I was not going to until I'd met something. I waited around by myself hoping something would turn up . . . My turn now. He was passing me very fast on my starboard side about three wing spans away . . . Unfortunately he was climbing fast and to keep my sights on, my nose had to be pulled high, bringing me to the stall and only the two starboard guns fired . . . The ME 109 flicked and for a moment I wondered if I'd hit him, but I saw no trace of hits on him and I think I missed . . . Stalling completely I went over in a vicious spin. Came out in a vertical dive . . . Eased back on the tail-trim and we flattened out O.K. at about 4,000 feet right over Hal Far aerodrome. Climbed up to about seven or eight thousand again and stooged around for a little, weaving this time O.K., but nothing attacked me and I saw nothing to attack. On approaching the aerodrome to land I saw three aircraft wrecked on it. Landed between them and saw 'C', My No. 1's aircraft up on its nose, the most spectacular. Found I was the only one of the four of us to return in one piece, though I had two explosive bullets through my starboard wing. Thanked God for my safe return. Apparently my luck was even better than I supposed for people saw my scrap with the 109 from the ground. Knight says the 109 had his No 2 with him behind me—there being three aircraft, and that No 2 followed me down in my spin a little way. He probably thought I was finished, as did those on the ground, when I span. The starboard main plane has to be changed. One of the bullets pierced the main span; however it stood up to a vertical dive with a full throttle."

So ended Oliver's first combat. He was to be victorious in many more; but to record them would degrade a picture into a catalogue. So before closing this interlude, for it is intended to be no more, simply the account of what one English boy accomplished for England and for Malta, one or two incidents may be selected. The bombs continued to fall, the fighters to fight. On the 10th January, 1942, Oliver had an interesting conversation with his new Commanding Officer, who, to his great joy, had started his career as a trooper in the Life Guards. "I was overjoyed to find that my C.O.'s views exactly coincided with mine, in that though each of us considers that the Air Force is the service to be in today in modern war, each wishes that times might go back to days of old, when we might have taken the field with the cavalry. That we would have loved more than this . . . Oh for the days that are gone! Oh for a horse not a Hurricane!"

On Sunday, 1st February, 1942, Oliver went to church. He was not impressed. "I don't know whether I'm religious. I am something very strongly; but I fear it is that I am superstitious. Is it superstition that makes me say my prayers at night regularly, always, and on certain occasions at odd moments throughout the day as well? Is it superstition or conscience—or what's the difference?—that has made me at times go alone to church? . . . And there are many religions. How can one really tell which is right: or are they all right? Scientifically is there a God? Then superstition cries: 'Don't doubt; it is unsafe.' If there is no God, and one believes in one, no harm will come of the error. But if there is a God and you don't believe it, awful things might happen."

Oliver amused his superiors by shouting 'Tally ho' over the wireless when he spotted an enemy—but they congratulated him on his daring when he landed.

Early in February Oliver was posted to Ta Qali, and so his Mess was in the very house in which I write. He was befriended by a Maltese nobleman across the way, whose daughter was very kind to him—she called him 'Baby'. (In the squadron he was known as Sonny "because I am so young and look younger".) Often he would be bidden to go into the walled garden and pick oranges, which were afterwards given him to eat. Whenever I pass that open door, which is almost every day, and look through into the garden, where those same trees are laden with fruit which glows 'like golden lamps in a green night', I think of the skilled young hand that plucked them so long ago.

Oliver's attitude to death has already been touched upon. To him it was just a hazard of the chase. But he was much afflicted by the loss of his friend James Stuart, with whom he had been an exact contemporary at Wellington. Later on he lost another. He devotes touching paragraphs to their memory. He felt impelled to visit their graves, in the town of Cospicua. The bombing had been frightful. Hal Far had been so badly battered that one shelter, Oliver records on the 27th March was beyond clearing. It was simply sealed up, with the corpses inside it, and a funeral service held over what had now become a mass grave. Decorations, he says had to be announced as speedily as possible or the recipients would be dead before they learned of them. With Greek irony, Oliver learned that he had been awarded the Distinguished Flying Cross on the 18th April.

He would often visit friends in hospital, and enemies as well. The scene is Imtarfa, on Wednesday, the 1st April. After calling on his wounded friends, "I spoke to the German pilot whom I met there on my previous visit. We got on very well. I told him how much I would like to have been in the *Luftwaffe*, especially to fight the Russians. He said it was great fun fighting the Russians, one being able to destroy usually four or five aircraft a day. He was disappointed that he had not joined his squadron before it left Russia. He also tried to show me the trick of the ME 109 on landing. Imaginary Messerschmidts made landings all over the bed, some putting in a wing, because the pilot held off too high, and some because he let his speed drop too low, and others because the pilot pulled back too hard on the 'stick'." The previous visit had been on the 19th March. "It was he who shot down a Spitfire yesterday and was then shot down by MacQueen. He's a friendly fellow and quite amusing The Mdina Mess is full of his sayings but we were unable to speak to him long as we were turned out by the orderly. Waved him good-bye and he waved back. Apparently he wanted to congratulate the pilot who shot him down and did so when MacQueen visited him. He was very pleased when they confirmed that he had destroyed the Spitfire quite regardless of the fact that it was one of the friends of his visitors that he'd killed. He asked them to telegraph the *Luftwaffe* in Sicily that he had shot it down in case his No. 1 had not seen it, as previously he was the baby of the squadron, which he had joined a month ago and the only one who had not shot down anything. Apparently his squadron had 196 victories to its credit. His C.O. has forty victories, and his No. 1 on this last flight was a man with twenty-eight victories. Before coming to Sicily his squadron had been in Russia. It had been in various campaigns including the Battle of Britain, so it appears that at least one of the enemy squadrons here is one of their best. Previous to this fellow's victory, it had shot down four aircraft of ours in this area. On hearing there was a shortage of toothpaste here, the captive observed that he was sure the *Luftwaffe* in Sicily would drop some cases of toothpaste for us from a Junkers 88."

How endearing, how revealing, how relevant, this bedside chat between the English and German 'babies'!

The Mess, the airfields, the hospital wards, the corpses—yes, often enough. But only once does Oliver record a visit to a cemetery, to the graves of his two friends Stuart and Macnamara—in Cospicua, a town unknown to him.

Tuesday, 17th March, 1942

"From Casa Paula Square, I took the Cospicua road. Cospicua is a place I've never been before, though I've mentioned it in my diary, having at one time thought Casa Paula to be Cospicua.

"I went through meandering streets in the Three Cities and the road sometimes ran through tunnels below the old battlements. I passed bomb craters and demolished houses and eventually a policeman gave me a small boy for a guide. We threaded our way for some distance along the bottom of an old fosse where people live like rabbits in holes and hutches, driven there by the bombs of the Third Reich—a messy place, this fosse, man and chicken, dog and cat, all intermingled. The boy brought me out the other end and I gave him 4d.

"A policeman now directed my steps to the wrong place. Climbed a steep hill and then had to retrace my steps again. Eventually I found an old lane under the directions of the inhabitants and came to the cemetery.

"An old Maltese labourer, the chief gravedigger it seemed showed me the registration book and I found the names of James Stuart and Macnamara poor dears. Macnamara was buried nearest the gate in grave No 90. Then I found Stuart's grave, No 15, and was rather disgusted to find him and another fellow, a pilot officer from Kalafrana, were buried in the same grave. I was sorry to see the graves so bare, no cross, no name, just a number. The old Maltese explained that all that would be attended to after the war and that for the present the tombstone markers were all employed in government work and that anyway since war with Italy, the marble supply had been cut. Think they might at least have wooden crosses. Gave the old man 10/- and instructed him to take especial care of these two graves. He promised that he would procure flowers for them this very day."

Sunday, 19th April, 1942

"Yes! I have been awarded the D.F.C. Today being Sunday, I must wait until tomorrow to go to Valetta to send my mother a cable and to buy the ribbon."

That was the last entry in the war diary of Pilot-officer Oliver Ormrod, D.F.C., aged twenty years and three days. No-one knew how he died, only that he was dead, killed in combat.

. . .

Not long ago, I was calling on Mr Michael Kissaun, the Manager of Malta's National Theatre, built by Grand Master Manoel de Vilhena in 1731, and one of the most beautiful in Europe.

"Michael," I said, "I have just been reading the war diary of a young English boy, who fought here—from November 1941 until April 1942. He was a pilot. He was shot down. He was only twenty."

"You mean Oliver Ormrod, Stewart?"

"Well, yes I do—but how on earth do you know?"

"I found his body: it was on the top of a house."

"Where?"

"Cospicua."

10

NADIR

1942

In the last chapter an attempt was made to see the war, just a few months of it, as it was viewed by thousands on both sides, as a personal combat, a tournament in which personal honour and patriotism must at all hazards be vindicated, and in which the forfeit for the supreme prize of life itself might well be death.

But from Oliver Ormrod's astonishingly detailed diary, some aspects of major strategy emerge; behind the endearing buoyancy of youth lurk the crushing burdens of battle. Indeed they did.

We learn that the German Air Force was back in Sicily, and that some of their most experienced and skilful pilots were under orders to 'suppress' Malta. We learn, too, how successful they were in wrecking the principal airfields, so that it was more and more necessary to rely on such subsidiary strips as Ta Qali. Unsuitable as this was in many ways, it had the advantage that there are no buildings within about half a mile of it. Thus Mdina, where Oliver's Mess was billeted, escaped almost unscathed. Nevertheless at the Point de Vue hotel, only just outside its Main Gate, twelve pilots who were housed there were killed by the explosion of a single bomb. At last, we learn, Spitfires had reached Malta. The first consignment of fifteen arrived, flown in from the veteran *Eagle*, which had set out from Gibraltar on the 7th March. Sixteen more followed on the 21st and the 29th March. Forty-six more were flown in from the United States carrier *Wasp* on the 20th May; yet so utterly inadequate was the aircraft-housing in Malta, even then, that within three days the German *Fliegerkorps II* had destroyed or damaged almost all of them *on the ground*, and only six fighters remained serviceable. On the

9th May, sixty more were flown from the *Wasp* and the *Eagle*: this time the ground-crews proved so efficient that many of the aircraft were in action within thirty-five minutes of their arrival. On the following day, Kesselring reported to Berlin that "the neutralisation of Malta was complete". Just how accurate was Kesselring's estimate? Once again we are faced with the puzzling paradox: neither side knew how badly the other was faring, and neither seemed able to correct its own proven errors.

In December 1941, the whole balance of naval power in the Mediterranean had been reversed by a daring Italian exploit. The development by the Italians of 'chariots' or 'pigs'—one-man submarines, has already been mentioned. It had been known for years that the Italians specialised in this brave and lethal form of warfare. As early as 1935, Tesei (who alas was never seen again after the M.T.B. attack on Malta already described) and a colleague called Toschi had perfected their apparatus, and Italian submarines had been specially adapted to carry the 'chariots' to within striking distance of their targets. One of these submarines was sunk, and its crew taken prisoner; but they kept their secret. Another, at its fourth attempt, sank three merchant ships in Gibraltar harbour.

On the night of the 18th December, 1941, Commander Borghese brought his submarine to the surface only a mile and two furlongs distant from the lighthouse on Alexandria mole. Into the harbour slipped three 'chariots'. All three 'jockeys' were veterans of the exploits at Gibraltar. Luck was on their side, because the net-defence was opened to admit them. Actually it had been breached to let in some destroyers of Admiral Vian's force, but in the darkness the Italians came in as well, narrowly escaping being run down by the destroyers. The target of one of the chariots was the battleship *Valiant*. After an astonishing struggle, in which his 'chariot' plunged to the bottom, De la Penne succeeded in affixing his giant torpedo to the bottom of the vessel. He then swam to the mooring buoy, from which, together with his assistant, he was taken prisoner. Once again, the Italians' lips remained sealed. Confined in the hold, knowing when the time fuse was due to go off, they were actually still in their dark captivity when the great battleship blew up, and sank until she rested on the bottom. A few minutes earlier Martellotta's warhead had blown the stern off the tanker *Sagona*, and had seriously damaged the destroyer *Jervis* which was lying aside. Martellotta and his companion reached shore but were arrested at the dockyard gate. Meanwhile Luigi de la Penne had reached the deck of the ruined *Valiant*, just in time to witness the explosion which made a mere hulk of the Fleet Flagship, the historic *Queen Elizabeth*, on board which had been signed the surrender of the German High Seas Fleet in 1918. Marceglia and his companion made good their escape, and set out for the submarine which was waiting for them off Rosetta; but were betrayed by one of those minor accidents which so often overthrow great designs. They had been supplied, thoughtfully enough, with money; but it was English money, five pound notes, which were no longer current in Egypt. So they, too, were arrested.

As opera, this exploit was superb: Verdi never set a more dramatic libretto. But viewed in the theatre of war, by the English, it was a major disaster. To quote Macintyre again: "Thus six brave and resourceful men eliminated at one stroke Cunningham's battle-squadron at a time when replacements were not available. For, eleven days before, the Japanese delivered their treacherous attack on Pearl Harbour. The battleship *Prince of Wales* and battle-cruiser *Repulse* had gone down before the torpedo aircraft of the Japanese Navy. With what remained of her naval strength Britain turned to defend her eastern Imperial possessions."

It appeared that all was up with England in the Mediterranean. But once again the paradox emerges from the fog. The Italian fleet were still determined to avoid any major engagement with the Royal Navy, even though at that time its striking force in the Eastern Mediterranean was reduced to three light cruisers, the anti-aircraft cruiser *Carlisle*, some destroyers, and, at Malta the cruiser *Penelope*. (The *Ajax* was there too, but was out of action.) The Italians had four battleships, three heavy and three light cruisers, and a far larger number of destroyers and submarines than we had. But the Italians had one object—to protect the vital convoys which sustained their armies in North Africa: Malta, it was decided, could be left to the

Luftwaffe. Thus it happened that more convoys did in fact reach Malta. To cite Macintyre once more. "It must not be thought that this brief period in January 1942 when the replenishment and reinforcement of Malta went on unimpeded was a period of British control of the central Mediterranean. Simultaneously with the re-opening of the sea-route from Alexandria to Malta as the result of the Eighth Army's advance, *Fliegerkorps* had gone into action, striking particularly hard at the airfields of Malta whenever an Italian convoy operation was in progress. Thus at this time each side was finding itself able to use the central Mediterranean for its own purposes, but, unable to prevent the enemy from using it, neither side could claim to control it."

Malta's supreme ordeal was now about to begin. How it was to end is one of the most dramatic episodes of the whole war. It was, quite literally a matter not merely of days, but of hours.

Here, in brief are the factors in the situation. First Britannia no longer ruled the waves of the Mediterranean. Secondly, Rommel in North Africa and *Fliegerkorps II* in Sicily had reduced Malta to an isolation which brought disaster, that is to say, defeat and surrender, daily nearer. Not only were the airfields battered to mud and rubble, not only were the soldiers and airmen worn out, the dockyard hands exhausted, but everyone was hungry.

Whatever shortcomings there may have been in the supply of aircraft and in the proper accommodation for them, the provision of adequate food supplies had been tackled with expert foresight, and continued to be so directed throughout the war. It was, in fact, a major factor in the Island's final victory. The 'capable young Australian' mentioned by Mrs Norman, now Sir Robert Jackson of the World Health Organisation, informed me in a recent letter that "the preparation of the fortress for the siege was simply one aspect of the wider pattern of the defence plan and the general scheme of rearmament—all of which were accomplished successfully."

The granaries were replenished, and every available acre put under cultivation. This whole activity sprang from "roots bedded in the Munich crisis", Sir Robert tells me. Even so, not every contingency could be foreseen. For instance, in 1942 the area under wheat was approximately 12,000 acres, a very big increase on the pre-war figure, and yet only sixty per cent of the 1918 acreage of 20,000 acres? What had caused this damaging decline? Simply an economic fact. During the period between the two wars, Italian and French viticultural processes had been introduced into the Island, with the result that a large proportion of wheat-bearing land had been transformed into far more profitable vineyards. (Malta wines nowadays are of excellent quality, and are to be obtained on the London market.) Or take potatoes. I cite Mr Leslie Oliver's excellent *Malta Besieged.*

"In 1938 the Island was able to export 24,000 tons." Many of these went to Holland, in which country a type of large potato, produced in plenty in Malta, had long been popular: it was in fact a staple export. "And in 1941 the production was such that in order to stabilise prices and minimise wastage, it was found necessary to include a large percentage of potato in the island's bread. In 1942 there was such a tremendous change in the situation that it was found necessary to prohibit the sale of potatoes except to the Government, which purchased the whole crop at a price which was virtually a subsidy, and re-issued the potatoes to the public at a much lower price and on a ration basis." Despite the action of the Government—and their measures were extremely efficient, with expert dieticians in charge—prices inevitably soared, and what the French, with Gallic delicacy call 'a parallel market', came into existence. Only the other day, a Maltese lady, asking me over an excellent supper whether I was going to write about the hunger during the siege, said "How well I remember paying twopence for two beans!"

The decline in the potato crop, like so many of the factors which contributed to the hunger, was due to the enemy. Maltese farmers used to import about 4,000 tons of seed potatoes every year, most of which came from Great Britain. (Potatoes will not germinate in Malta's rocky soil, so the seed must be imported.) Early in 1942, a whole consignment was sunk, and substitute tubers brought from Cyprus germinated but poorly in Malta's soil. The plain, sad fact was that the Axis now had the upper hand. Mr Galea's statistics tell their own shocking tale. During the last ten days of December 1941 alone, civilian casualties were more than fifty. In January, 1942, nearly eighty people perished, in February some 200. March and April were both months of horror. By then citizens were excavating 'cubicles' even in the walls of the fosse which separates Mdina from Rabat: their blocked-up entries can still be seen beneath the flowers of the Howard Gardens. The general effect of such brutal assaults may be gathered from Mr Galea's summary: Altogether Malta had 3,343 alerts, which accounted for 2,357 hours and six minutes. It is believed that some 16,000 tons of bombs were dropped. The number of buildings of all kinds destroyed or damaged was between 30,000 and 40,000. April 1942 was Malta's worst month. No less than 5,715 bombers attacked her, 1,638 in one week, and 590 bombs were dropped on the three aerodromes in one day: on another day the same three targets received 615 bombs. It really did seem as though Malta was being 'suppressed'. The total tonnage of bombs dropped on Malta during April 1942, namely 6,728, was roughly the equivalent of thirty-six attacks on Coventry.

Never were the anti-aircraft defences more grimly and effectively employed than during this purgatory. Here again, the sense of 'time lost' overcomes the modern visitor, just as it does when he contemplates the blocked-up refuges in the Rabat Fosse. Like Mr Michael Kissaun of the Manoel Theatre, Major Gerald Amato-Gauci, the Manager of Thos. Cook & Son in Kingsway, might easily be mistaken for a professor at the University. And yet this kind and courteous man, we read, was in charge of an anti-aircraft battery on the 11th January. There were several attacks that day, during one of which a bomb exploded within five yards of Lieutenant (as he then was) Amato-Gauci, wounding him in the chin and neck. "Although shocked and in great pain he carried on with the control of the guns, shouting out the necessary orders. He refused to receive first aid until the raid was over, when he had to be helped to the post, and subsequently admitted to hospital. This officer's staunch devotion to duty and great display of coolness set a very high example to all the men under his command. After his return from hospital, and during deliberate attacks by the enemy on his position [which was in the thick of it, just above the Grand Harbour] he has always shown great initiative in dealing with the situation and his conduct has been an inspiration to all his men."

It was conduct of this sort, which earned the Military Cross for Major Amato-Gauci, this toughness of fibre, this devotion to discipline and duty, that enabled the Maltese nation to survive. To quote the simple and eloquent words of Mr E. S. Tonna: "Nobody would have imagined that the first blow would be so devastating in its effects. It was the first day of March 1942 and Floriana was still unscathed with the exception of one single scar – my own house. The sweet breezes of the approaching season were lulling the whole District, and most of the inhabitants were having the usual after-meal stroll along the wide open spaces of Floriana, basking in the midday sunshine. The Sword of Damocles was impending over all. The Air Raid was sounded, and the Red Flag was hoisted. The shelters became overcrowded and the bastions came to life with spectators watching the convoy ships serenely moored in the Grand Harbour, whilst the din of the enemy aircraft was faintly heard in the distance.

"All of a sudden the skies rained death, and the heavy missiles hit one of the most thickly populated sections of the District. I instantly rushed to the stricken area to be met by a ghastly sight. I knew who the victims must have been and was not wrong in my conjecture: Miss Pulo would not come to the school tomorrow and be bothered with the daily notes and shaping of figures; Joe a young pupil would not sing and relate stories to divert his young colleagues in the school-shelter . . . This was the story of Malta being written in blood."

And yet Mr Tonna makes this touching comment: "We wept at the time and regretted the ordeal; but we were and are equally proud that it happened for otherwise Malta would have had a different story to relate to her posterity, would have witnessed a world tragedy without her own sorrowful aspects and would have listened to an epic devoid of the brave deeds of her heroic sons."

On the 15th February, 1942, the *Times of Malta* under the heading 'The Malta Front' carried the news: "City suffers casualties." A cinema (the Regent in Kingsway) which was crowded with servicemen and civilians, received a direct hit and the exact number of casualties was never published; but it is known to have been high.

In the same raid the Casino Maltese, next to the Regent, was hit and partially wrecked. Several members and staff were killed.

It was this dire emergency of February that brought about the introduction of the famous Victory Kitchens, or communal feeding-centres. On the 3rd March, Sir Edward Jackson, introducing the Third War Budget, said that in the Committee stage of the Bill they would ask for a vote for the organisation of community cooking, the principal object of which was economy in fuel and the desirability of feeding the population from centralised sources. It was not possible at the moment to say how far income would cover the expenditure on the scheme. He would propose to insert in the Estimates a sum of £25,000 to carry on until they could see more clearly.

On the 11th March, the *Times of Malta* announced that as from the following day, a Victory Kitchen would be opened in College Street, Rabat.

The kitchens multiplied quickly. On the 15th May, Mr (later Sir Andrew) Cohen in answer to Mr Valenzia's move in the Council of Government to institute a Mobile Canteen Corps said that the answer was communal feeding. They already had twenty-three kitchens all over the country and nineteen more were to be opened that month. Each centre served about 200 people, and there would have been many more if they did not have to give up half their rations.

As moving and reinacting as any of the stories of those terrible days I find that which Dr George Borg, M.D., related to me in his home at Luqa.

In April 1942 German bombers had swept in wave after wave in their attempt to annihilate Malta—5,715 bombers, and 6,700 tons of bombs, the equivalent of the Coventry blitz repeated every eighteen hours for thirty days.

On Sunday, 19th April, after attending the 8 o'clock Mass, Dr Borg's father, a widower of forty-eight, asked his two sons, George, then aged eighteen and his younger brother Gawdenz, a nine-year-old, whether they would like to go out with him. Mr Borg, like so many Maltese today, loved to spend a Sunday morning driving a fine pony in a light cart, or 'spider'. Both boys were a bit apprehensive, but George, seeing how keen his father was to spend a traditional Sunday morning, said 'with some bravado' as he recalls, "Never mind about the raids, I'll go with you, Dad." His delighted father bade the boy go and get the equipage ready. An alarm sounded, but George, scanning the sky, saw nothing and led the horse to the front of the house . . .

"We left our home at Gudja and I drove along the road girdling the harbour. After half an hour as we were trotting down the deserted streets of Pawla Hill, we heard the sound of ack-ack shells bursting in the distance. We hurried to cross Marsa wharf which was a dangerous spot. We saw the Stukas diving one after the other to bomb Dockyard Creek, about 300 yards away.

"Sensing imminent danger my father told me to drive to the abattoir air-raid shelter. I urged the horse on and he started with a fine gallop up the hill. My father smiling advised me not to be excited as it would make matters worse. When we arrived at the iron gate of the abattoir, I alighted, quickly took a rein out of the harness and tethered the horse to the iron door. My father stood looking on.

"All of a sudden I heard the whistling of a descending bomb—the sound increasing ominously. It dawned on me that a bomb was falling directly on us. Without a moment's hesitation I threw myself flat on the ground. Just as I was about to shout out a warning to my father I felt his body upon me and his hands clasping me tightly. My father was a six footer and his shoulders were over two feet wide.

"I had no chance to utter a word to him because a tremendous crack and a bright blinding light flashed just on my right, only four yards away.

"The acid smell of sulphur and the TNT, the burning dry taste in my mouth, the blurring of vision with the smoke and the dust, the hissing loud noise in my ears were a terrible experience which still haunts my dreams after twenty-six years.

"I then began to feel the weight of the stones and rubble pressing my legs and back to the ground. A thought stabbed my mind that I was going to be buried alive like some people I had seen under the debris of a house a week before. But luckily my head and arms remained uncovered. I brought my hands under my chest and pressed down firmly to push myself up. With three or four jerks I freed myself from the heap of stones but found that my right leg was heavy and numb. I had not felt any pain until then.

"My clothes were all torn away by the blast and I was left covered with only a few tatters. Blood was pouring from my left forearm and down both my legs.

"I coughed as the dryness in my mouth was very irritating and a mouthful of blood and dust came out. I coughed again and again and more blood came out. I thought this was it. I was going to die.

"Through the smoke and dust-filled air I tried to look around me and I was shocked to see that the horse and light cart had disappeared. As little by little the air began to clear, I found myself standing in a weird desolation.

"The previous scene had completely changed. Where the horse and light cart had been, there was only a large ugly hole in the street, and the houses on both sides lay in two large, scorched mounds of ruin. I felt very lonely.

"I saw my father lying face upwards about twelve yards in front of me. I limped towards him. His face was gaunt and his eyes glazed. He looked certainly worse than me. He could not stand up. His first words were that he was going to die.

"In heart-broken words I recited with him the Act of Contrition. In the middle he stopped and could not carry on. I encouraged him to continue and with difficulty he did so.

"I got very agitated and began to shout for help. The people inside the shelter which was fifty yards inside the abattoir came out to help us. Again bombs started whistling down as another wave of Stukas were diving on us, and the people ran and dragged me with them to the shelter, supporting me under the arms. In the confusion I was under the impression they were bringing my father to the shelter as well."

When, about ten minutes later, the bombing stopped, six men

went with George to where his father lay. "My father was lying as before, drenched with blood." George was almost deaf now, his ears filled with black burned powder and his ear-drums pierced with blast. He did his utmost to catch his father's words. "When he saw me, he told me in a faltering voice: 'George, I am dying, I am dying. I did my best to save you'."

Father and son were eventually conveyed to the casualty hospital. The journey through the battered and blocked streets took an hour. The last time he saw his father "he was gasping his last breath. I called him three times but he did not answer, and then I kissed his cold pale face smeared still with blood and dirt."

After a month, George was discharged from hospital. Now, a quarter of a century later, Dr George Borg, Ph.C., M.D., is one of Malta's most valued and respected citizens. It is hard, even when one sees the scars on his body and feels the deeper ones in his heart, to realise how his father died to save his eighteen-year-old son on that fatal Sunday morning. But Malta is like that.

Chapter after doeful chapter was added to the 'epic'. In Floriana alone, the Capuchin convent and the famous church of St Publius were wrecked, and other buildings reduced to rubble. The last big raid took place on the 8th May. Other parts of the Island suffered the same fate, notably Senglea and Vittoriosa. Vittoriosa was originally known as Birgu, the 'tower' or 'town' simply, but for its share in winning the victory against the Turks in 1565, La Valette had dubbed it 'Vittoriosa', the victorious. Hundreds of its defenders had been buried in the main square, others a foot or two below the ground where they had fallen. Whenever a new building was erected, old bones came to light. On the 16th January, 1941, during the ever-memorable battle for the *Illustrious*, Vittoriosa once more became a shambles. More than forty people, sheltering in a basement, were killed almost on the very same spot as the warriors of 1565 had been laid to rest. Today, on the 16th January, a mass is offered in St Lawrence's church for the repose of their souls.

"During these months, food had become very scarce, and lack of fuel cut off all supplies of gas and electricity, so the Victory Kitchens came into being. These provided one cooked meal a day to be collected at 12 noon or 5 in the afternoon. It was an amusing sight to see a long line of saucepans and pots outside the kitchen by nine in the morning. These pots formed the queue and no-one disputed their position. I remember our first meal. Carrie, our Maltese maid, took a large basin and we waited expectantly. She returned with three thin sausages and fifteen peas for the three of us. This, with a small bread ration, represented the main meal of the day. A half potato came twice a week. We had eaten all the goats and so there was no milk except for a few tins reserved for babies. So we eagerly awaited a consignment of powdered milk. When it came [probably by submarine] it consisted of two tablespoonfuls to last sixteen days. Fruit was plentiful, but was sold out when hundreds of thirsty soldiers besieged the baskets. There was no beer, and the most drastic form of intoxication was a bunch of grapes or a slice of melon. Of course, the Black Market crept in as everywhere and I remember a woman who told me she had given a suite of furniture for some potatoes. Eggs—if there were any—were 15/- a dozen. If anyone was leaving the Island the news always seemed to get around and crowds would arrive at the house to see if there was any chance of buying a few stores or clothes too for that matter. Some provision shops resorted to second-hand clothing displays on otherwise empty shelves. A friend of mine secured a rabbit for 17/6 and then couldn't get rid of the idea that it was really the shopkeeper's cat.

"Another thing we were short of was hot water, but we found an excellent idea was to put a tin bath of water on a flat roof in the early morning and leave the sun to do the rest. By mid-afternoon the water was warm enough to bathe in. If you wanted boiling water you had to look for wood from the bombed houses and boil the kettle gypsy fashion on a fire in the corner of the roof. Later on, even bombed wood was scarce and only Victory Kitchens were allowed to use it.

"For lighting we used a bootlace or piece of string, stuck into a potted meat jar containing a little paraffin; this was enough to light our way round the furniture. I remember an exciting game of 'Monopoly' played with two of these lights. During this time, I was teaching at the Royal Naval Dockyard School. The children were astonishing in their attitude. They were thrilled to watch and knew every type of plane or bomb, and the sound and position of all the guns. Even though their faces went a little pale when bombs were very near, they continued to come to school. One boy sometimes took one and a half to two hours to get there, with all the interruptions on the way—but come he would, and alone too . . .

"Our red letter day was Sunday, 10th May, 1942. Spitfires had arrived. It seemed that Jerry didn't know for, as usual, along came his JU 87's and 88's in waves of fifty or so, expecting to have an easy passage if they managed to elude the A.A. fire, but our Spitfires were up, and seemed to meet them head on. The sky was an absolute circus. Machines fell out of it like flies. Bursts of shell fire were so close that the sky looked like a wasp's nest and the seafront was lined with cheering crowds who forgot falling shrapnel and splinters in the sheer joy of witnessing a battle where we at last held our own and were superior; thirty-six enemy machines were brought down in an hour. Jerry got the fright of his life. That was the last of his mass attacks.

"And the spirit of the people never faltered, and the friendships of peacetime were more closely cemented by the hardships we all shared. I feel I could go back to Malta at any time, and find the Vellas, the Spiteris, the Mizzis, the Pisanis, the Asphars, the Torregianis and all the other Maltese families and greet them as comrades. Of course we all grumbled at times and wished the bread would cut into just a few more slices, but the perils and courage of the men who brought it to us turned our grumblings into thankfulness and humility. There was a wonderful confidence in what was being done here at home. All of us felt that our troubles were light if England was winning through. Crowds always gathered at the public loudspeakers to hear every bit of news and to await the great day when North Africa would be freed, for this would be our salvation, too. I almost wish we had been there when that day did come—we only missed it by a few weeks."

The siege affected even so stable and unemotional an institution as the Oxford and Cambridge examinations. The question papers were despatched in July, 1942. They only reached Malta in October.

The answers did not arrive in England until after Easter 1943. They bore interesting evidence of their origin. First, at the head of each boy's paper was a solemn declaration that he had not seen the questions before. Scattered in the text the words 'air raid', in brackets, showed the conditions in which the papers had been written. Most characteristic of all was, often enough, after a boy's name the proud addition, 'Gunner, Royal Malta Artillery', because in the interval between the end of the academic year and the date on which they sat for the examination, many of the lads had been called up.

With hunger and weariness came scabies, a foul disease of the skin. From his comfortable home in Detroit, George Grech still recalls those lean days. "We lost so much weight that my belt could go half way round my waist in excess. But I remember Mr Churchill's words when he said 'fasten up your belt until victory is achieved', and with God's help victory was achieved . . . During the siege what hurt us most was when all the family had the scabies. I had it on my hands, but also on my seat and I couldn't sit down. It was the lack of calories. I remember a working man had less than 2,000 calories a day . . . I remember our delight when the new A.O.C. Sir H. Lloyd ordered Spitfires for our defence and then we had planes that could beat the ME 109, and shoot down bombers before they approached the coastline. The situation was serious, very serious; but as far as I know I never heard of any Maltese who had in his mind that we should surrender. No, everyone I recall was determined that we should repay our enemies with the same coin they were paying us. And it really happened. Do you remember those 1,000 bomber raids over individual cities? They sure reaped what they sowed."

On the 15th April, 1942, King George VI awarded the George Cross to Malta. It was far more than a mere medal. It was the recognition by the Sovereign of the universal admiration of and gratitude for the heroism and devotion of the Maltese nation.

It was not until the 13th September, 1942, that Lord Gort who had succeeded General Dobbie as Governor, was able to present the Cross at a formal parade on the Palace Square to the Chief Justice, Sir George Borg, on behalf of the nation. Both the Cross and the citation are now preserved in the Palace. It was venerated as an eikon; and I have before me as I write the faded sheets containing the orders for its display in the different villages of the Island, so that every citizen should be physically aware of his share in the earning of it. By that time, Malta's ordeal was almost over; but when the Cross was awarded, her most cruel, critical trials were still in the future, and it is to the grand political scene that we must now return.

II

SAVING DISGRACE

1942

During the doleful days of the spring of 1942, it seemed that both sides were suffering from some sort of mental disorder, that neither could make up its mind to any definite course of action, or that having decided on a policy they had not the will to carry it out. On the English side, the inability of their naval and air forces either to protect their own convoys from attack or sufficiently to damage those of the enemy had led the Commanders-in-Chief to doubt whether they could try to go on attempting to supply Malta—which would have meant the death of the Island. On the Italian side, despite their command of the sea, and, with Kesselring's lethal support, of the sky as well, despite the reports they received of the Island's plight, divided counsels and hesitation still prevented their carrying out their so long, so meticulously prepared plan to invade the Island —*Operazione C3: Malta*. It is hard indeed for a layman, even with so many sources from both sides available to him, to unravel the cat's cradle of the 1942 campaigns, so various and vacillating were the policies and ploys of the chief participants.

Count Ciano's diary goes some way towards explaining Italian doubts and fears. As early as the 9th November, 1941 he had written: "Since 19th September, we had given up trying to get convoys through to Libya; every attempt had been very costly, and the losses suffered by our merchant marine had reached such proportions as to discourage any further experiments. Tonight we tried it again; Libya needs materials, arms, fuel, more and more every day. And a convoy of ships left, accompanied by two ten-thousand-ton cruisers and ten destroyers, because it was known that at Malta the

British had two battleships intended to act as wolves among the sheep. An engagement occurred the results of which are inexplicable. All, I mean *all*, our ships were sunk and one or maybe two or three destroyers . . . Under the circumstances we have no right to complain if Hitler sends Kesselering as commander in the south."

On the 22nd April, 1942, he writes: "The Duce informs me that Marshal Kesselring on his return from Germany brought Hitler's approval for the landing operation on Malta. It appears that the Island has been really damaged by aerial bombardments. This does not however alter the fact that the coastal defences are still intact. Therefore in the opinion of some naval experts, the undertaking is still dangerous and in any case would be expensive." Again, on the 28th April: "Cavallero talks to me much about the Malta operation. He realises it is a tough nut. The preparations under way are being made with maximum attention and care, and with the conviction that the attack is essential. But whether the operation will take place, or when, are other matters, and Cavallero makes no commitments. As is his nature he digs himself in behind a great quantity of ifs and buts."

On the 12th May he entered: "Cavallero outlines our programme for carrying on the war in the Mediterranean. At the end of the month Rommel will attack in Libya with the aim of defeating the British forces. If he can he will take Tobruk and will go as far as the old boundaries; if not he will limit himself to forestalling an attack by the enemy by striking first. Then all the forces will be concentrated for an attack on Malta. The Germans are sending a parachute division commanded by General Student and are furnishing us with technical material for the assault. It will take place in July or August at the latest. Afterwards it will no longer be possible because of the weather. Cavallero declares: 'I know that it is a difficult undertaking and that it will cost us many casualties, and I know too that I am staking my head on this undertaking. But I am the one who wants it because I consider it absolutely essential for the future development of the war. If we take Malta, Libya will be safe.' . . . Cavallero does not conceal the fact that he hopes to derive a great deal of

Ta Qali airfield (top right) today, from Oliver Ormrod's Mess, now Xara Palace Hotel. Below: defaced milestone still reads 'blank miles from blank'.

A contemporary lorry still recalls the famous American bomber. Below: H.M.S. *Illustrious* is remembered in the Palace Square.

personal glory from this operation. [Which he proposed to command in person.] But I believe he will never acquire it."

Colonel Casero, an old and trusted friend of Ciano's was chief of staff to Fougier, who commanded the Italian Air Force. On 13th May: Casero "does not share Cavallero's easy enthusiasms for the attack on Malta. Malta's anti-aircraft defence is still very efficient, and their naval defence is entirely intact. The interior of the Island is one solid nest of machine-guns . . . The landing of paratroops would be very difficult; a great part of the planes are bound to be shot down before they can deposit their human cargo. The same must be said for landings by sea. Again it must be remembered that two days of minor aerial bombardment by us only served to stiffen resistance. In these last attacks we, as well as the Germans, have lost many feathers. Even Fougier is anxious about a landing operation and the German General Lörzer did not conceal his open disagreement. The supporters of the undertaking are Kesselring and Cavallero, the latter going through his usual tricks to put the responsibility on the shoulders of others."

One final quotation from Ciano may be added, to show the moral atmosphere of the Duce's 'court' in its decline.

On the 19th May: "The English would like to send some hospital ships to Malta. Our Navy agrees in principle, but the Germans are against it. The Duce decides against it especially because his experience has taught him the many things it is possible to hide in hospital ships when the blockade would otherwise prevent their passage. *Last winter we were able to deliver some timely supplies of petrol to Benghazi by making use of white ships*"—i.e. ships of the Italian Red Cross.

But to one man the overall situation remained clear, the overriding necessity of maintaining Malta vital, and that man was Churchill. It is not always remembered that during the decade of his political eclipse, Churchill had spent much of his time and talent in compiling and publishing the biography of his ancestor the great Duke of Marlborough, who was in Wavell's expert opinion the greatest military commander in all history (with the Byzantine Belisarius 'equal first'). Churchill was accustomed therefore to think in terms of 'grand designs', of master policies, of world strategy. It came perfectly naturally to him. As it happened he knew Malta. As a young minister he had visited the Island, and like many young men had endeared himself to its inhabitants and them to him by getting on the right side of the 'wrong people'. He never forgot Malta; but he now realised that, sentiment apart, Malta had a vital rôle to play in winning the war. As early as June 1941, he had written: "You may be sure we regard Malta as one of the master-keys of the British Empire."

It must be remembered that the Italian Air Force had in fact suffered severe losses at the hands of the defenders of Malta. Franco Pagliano, in *Storia di diecimilia aeroplani*, admits that no Italian pilot expected to survive more than seven sorties over the Island. General Aldo Remondino, lately retired Chief of Staff of the Italian Air Force and a fighter pilot during the war, cheerfully attributes his white hair to his wartime experiences. "I grew old in no time over Malta," he said in a conversation with H. E. Mr Philip Pullicino, Ambassador of Malta to the Quirinal.

But Malta's situation now grew daily more desperate. Both sides knew it. On the 15th January the Italian Intelligence reported: "In consequence of the repeated air attacks on Malta, the population is profoundly depressed. Many a time the people are compelled to remain in inadequate cover for twenty hours and more. The attacks continue, fear, uncertainty and the tainted air produce among the individuals a sort of psychology of fear: they then run out into the street simply in order to be able to breathe pure air and to see the sky . . . The aerodromes of Ta Qali, Luqa and Hal Far are the objectives which have suffered most from these attacks. Also, the Harbour has been seriously damaged; and in particularly the basins of French Creek and Dockyard Creek have been rendered unusable. The hills surrounding the aforementioned airfields have been adapted as aircraft-garages [Those at Ta Qali are still clearly visible to this day, blocked up and sinister amid the gentle narcissus that star the slopes] and from these, in the case of an alarm, the English pursuit-planes set out. Many times however, so swift are the attacks, they are machine-gunned by low-level flying while they are getting ready to leave. Nearly all of what were at one time public shelters, and have not been destroyed, have been requisitioned and adapted for use as petrol-stores [The railway-tunnel beneath Rabat-Mdina was one such: it is now a mushroom-farm] and as repair-shops . . . As a result of the continuous attacks, Malta has lost much of its importance as a naval and air base. All the inhabitants are asking whether the forces of the Axis are contemplating the destruction or the invasion of the Island. Malta lives today under the incubus of invasion. The opinion is that the conference which took place at Garmisch between Grand Admiral Raeder and Admiral Riccardi had as its object the details of the invasion plan. It is certain that the population will not be able to resist actual attacks and the consequent moral depression."

Already, on the 3rd January, Vice-Admiral Ford, in charge in Malta, had written to Cunningham: "I've given up the number of raids we are getting. At the time of writing, 4 p.m., we have had exactly seven bombing raids since 9 a.m., quite apart from a month of all-night efforts. The enemy is definitely trying to neutralise Malta's effort, and, I hate to say, is gradually doing so. They have bust a sad number of our bombers and fighters etc., and must continue to do so . . ." Admiral Ford then asks for modern fighters, to be despatched either via Takoradi, in West Africa, or flown off from carriers. He continues: "Minesweeping is now difficult, and they appear to be laying them everywhere . . . Work in the yard is naturally very much slowed up as the result of the constant raids."

The reference to Garmisch, in the Italian intelligence report, is of great interest. Garmisch is a town on the Borders of Germany and Austria, not far from Oberammergau, and there on the 14th and 15th January, 1942, there took place a conference between the naval commanders of the Axis, Grand Admiral Raeder and the Italian Chief of Naval Staff, for a direct exchange of views on problems connected with the conduct of the war in the Mediterranean. (But how could such accurate information of the conference and its object have reached Malta so quickly? Probably two or more reports have been condensed into one: the final text is dated the 21st February, and the first part of it at any rate is said to have been furnished by 'a trustworthy source, via North Africa and France'). The first topic discussed was the necessity for keeping the Axis forces in North Africa supplied: in recent months they had suffered appalling losses from our naval and air forces, predominantly from submarine attacks. Now that it was clear that Franco was not going to involve Spain in the war, an attack on Gibraltar was out of the question. Tunisia was similarly barred by German unwillingness to exasperate the Vichy collaborators. So far both the commanders were in agreement. Moreover, as Raeder pointed out, it was almost certain that the Anglo-American forces in the Far East would for some time remain on the defensive, and would concentrate their naval forces in the Atlantic and the Mediterranean. Therefore, both admirals were in accord that their first object must be "the maintenance and reinforcement of positions in Libya", as they were also that this should be accomplished by the 'neutralisation' of Malta by air-attacks, and the encirclement of the Island by mine-fields, and other unspecified 'insidious means'. But there the agreement ended. The Italians claimed that nothing but the occupation of the Island could effect its *permanent* elimination, and that to that end the help of her ally was essential.

Her ally refused to give it. A joint committee was set up to discuss the matter. Despite the fact that Raeder was known to be in agreement with the Italian Navy on the feasibility, indeed the necessity, of occupying Malta, the German command took a contrary view. For one thing, they distrusted the Italian army—it had not done so well in North Africa, to say the least of it; secondly the German losses incurred in the capture of Crete made the German High Command reluctant to risk another similar adventure; thirdly Malta was known to be 'armed to the teeth', 'the strongest place in Europe', with powerful armaments concentrated in a very limited area, unlike those of Crete; fourthly, and decisively, they knew that Hitler shared their views. So, once again, 'C3' was shelved.

Hitler, like Napoleon before him, never understood sea-power. He considered that a first-rate army, backed by a first-rate air force, could win a war. And had he not been proved triumphantly right? Had not his might prevailed in France, in the Low Countries, in

Scandinavia, in North Africa, in Russia itself? Why, then worry about a little speck of rock in the Mediterranean, which had besides now passed out of English control?

A month later however, Hitler had partly, but only partly, changed his view. On the 13th February, he received Raeder in "an exceptionally friendly and cordial interview". The day before, the two German battle-cruisers *Scharnhorst* and *Gneisenau*, in company with the cruiser *Prinz Eugen* had made their way from Brest, through the Channel, right up to the North Sea, under the very noses of the English, and that exploit "had made the War Lord rather more benevolent than usual in his meetings with the Navy". With great tact and caution, Raeder began by making a *tour d'horizon* of all the maritime fronts of the world conflict. He explained his dispositions in regard to the Norway coast, discussed the battle of the Atlantic and the enemy convoys to Russia, and then, profiting from the well-disposed attitude of his interlocutor, worked his way round to the Mediterranean. Now, he pointed out, was the time to strike there. Events in the Far East had made it more than probable that Japan would occupy Ceylon. The Axis had only to join up with her, by way of Egypt, and England would be deprived of her vital oil supplies.

Hitler appeared to be impressed by this argument. Raeder went on to explain that victory in the Mediterranean depended on two factors (on which as it happened the British Admiralty were in perfect agreement with him): sea power and aero-naval-ground cooperation. The navy could not work without the bases which the army must seize and hold; the army could not operate without the help and protection of the air arm, and that in its turn depended on the navy for supplies and on the army for its bases. Mediterranean strategy, therefore, must co-ordinate these three arms to ensure success; sea power which secured the supplies which secured the bases, the bases which secured the sea power. The key to this circle is a central base to serve as a starting-point, and by far the most important base in the Mediterranean is the island-fortress of Malta. Malta, Raeder was careful to add, was not the final objective in the Mediterranean, merely the most important and urgent. He produced statistics to show how Axis losses at sea had notably decreased since the *Luftwaffe* had taken a hand. He ended by affirming that Malta, and Malta alone, was the keystone of the enemy's power in the Mediterranean, and therefore urged its "definitive annulment by occupation".

Hitler said he would think it over: first of all, the air-offensive must be stepped up, with the object of achieving neutralisation. Stepped up it was, and neutralisation was perilously close. While the Italians were training their landing forces, and studying every bay, creek and inlet not only of Malta but of Gozo, even of Comino as well, the *Luftwaffe* hammered at Malta, and the mine-fields were laid. As already related, even the steel morale of the people and garrison of Malta was beginning to show signs of fatigue. A comparison with 1941 will show how desperate the situation had become. In 1941, approaching from both east and west thirty-one transports had set out for Malta of which all save one arrived. In January 1942, a convoy arrived successfully from Alexandria. In February another convoy of three merchantmen was wiped out. In March another convoy approached from the east. It was accompanied by five cruisers, eighteen destroyers, five submarines (which were now being used as transports even; and I well remember receiving letters in Baghdad which had reached the Levant by submarine from Malta). The convoy consisted of five merchantmen. Three of the cruisers were damaged. Three of the destroyers were sunk, two damaged. One submarine was sunk. Only three of the four merchantmen reached Valetta, *and they were all sunk as they lay alongside the quay*. In retrospect it is almost beyond belief that the Grand Harbour was not yet fitted with smoke apparatus (which had already been installed in remote oil installations in Mesopotamia, and of which the Italians were known to have a particular horror). Worse, no precise arrangements had been made for the rapid unloading of the ships, and the speedy conveyance of their precious freight to places of safety. "That's not important." "This can wait." The result was that of the 26,000 tons which had actually arrived in starving Malta, only 5,000 were landed. The destruction of a ship is always tragic. Not only because so many brave and helpless men, gentle husbands and long-awaited fathers perish in cold misery, but because with them go down so many hours of labour, so much skill, so much hope and trust, so much strength and protection as well. The canon of Greek tragedy that violence must never be seen on the stage, only reported, was the product of Greek humanity. The Maltese are a humane nation. To see those cherished ships, and with them so much succour for themselves and their children, destroyed before their eyes, harrowed their souls. During that awful summer, two more convoys were assembled, one from the west and one from the east, both in the month of June. That from the west was escorted by no less than thirty-nine warships of all kinds. The convoy consisted of ten ships. Of the warships, two were sunk, and five damaged. Of the ten merchantmen only two reached Malta. The eastern convoy was a total failure. Of the seventy escorting warships, five were sunk, and five damaged. Of the eleven merchantmen, two were sunk, and one was damaged. The rest had to return to Alexandria. Not a single transport reached Malta.

For the citizens of Malta, these were indeed terrible days, the beginning of the final affliction. Miss Lydia Mary Galea, the daughter of a well-known Maltese artist, recalls how things went from bad to worse. In June 1940 the family went to Naxxar. Miss Galea was working in the Ordnance department in St John's Cavalier Valetta, in a shelter which was fifty feet below the ground. At first like others, her family did not live in the shelters. Then her father was killed, her aunt smothered. Miss Galea worked on. Gradually the shops which had been open in 1940, closed. There was no trade. Stocks were exhausted. The Victory Kitchens supplied one hot meal a day, generally of goat's meat. There was no sugar, and but little tea. One slice of bread with perhaps a little tomato sauce. Miss Galea, too, remembers the scabies, and the lice as well. There were queues even for water, because there was insufficient fuel available to keep the pumps running efficiently. It was even said that some people collected weeds from the Hastings Gardens and cooked them on such improvised stoves as they could contrive, from timber from bombed houses. "But we were determined to carry on, just like London. The naval officers would visit us and cheer us up. If we felt the blast of a bomb, they would say: 'It's windy down here; mind you don't catch cold'."

Miss Strickland, in a broadcast interview which she gave to Mr Macdonald Hastings of the B.B.C. in September 1943, when she was in London for a bit of rest tells her own graphic story.

Miss Strickland. I was born in Malta and resident there.

H. Including the siege?

S. Yes, right through from the beginning to the end.

H. And now that Malta's struggle is over, you've come to this country to see what we are up to?

S. Yes, and to have a rest . . . I must say it's really moving to see the intense personal interest in Malta which so many British people have. This was brought back to me happily when I was going over a war factory in the north. The porter who handed me my pass said, "I must have that back when you go out." I said, "No you won't. I must take it back to Malta." He said, "Malta. Give my love to Valetta and Floriana. I was there in *Euryalus* in 1900. I'm seventy-five now: some of my happiest times were spent in that Island."

H. And there must be thousands like that man. After all, Malta has been one of the Fleet's bases in the Mediterranean since . . .

S. Since Nelson came to the help of the Maltese insurgents against Napoleon in 1800.

H. When Malta became British?

S. That's right.

H. Well, Miss Strickland, it's the last three years we want to hear about tonight.

S. Well, Malta's war struggle for survival began with Italy's entry into the war. Britain reinforced the Island with troops, both infantry and gunners, and the Maltese Territorial Regiment was embodied.

H. And the R.A.F.

S. Well, they fought their first air battles over Malta by manning four naval Gladiator planes. But in August 1940, Britain reinforced us with twelve Hurricanes which she could ill spare. And it fought the Italians at odds of twenty to one. In the spring of 1941, they had to call in the *Luftwaffe* to help them which infuriated the Maltese.

H. Yes, I remember. That was the battle when they were repairing the *Illustrious.*

S. Malta won that battle but three of her cities, Vittoriosa, Senglea and Cospicua lay in ruins by the time the *Illustrious* was ready. The dockyard grimly moved underground into the living rock, soft yellow limestone rock that trembles and vibrates under direct hits but does not yield. "Just like a thousand snakes running round my stomach", was how a dockyard foreman summed up his experience. "Full fifteen minutes of direct hits and all Senglea down on top of us."

H. But what we'd like to know is how ordinary people in Senglea —and throughout Malta—got on during those early raids.

S. People found refuge with their uncles and aunts in other towns and villages. In Malta the family is always the unit, and some families grew to most uncomfortable proportions, thirty, forty and more as they crowded together. Eventually every village and town in the Island had its bomb scars; but as time passed, over thirteen miles of shelters were tunnelled by hand with axes out of the rock.

H. And did you sleep in these shelters?

S. Most people did, but we carried on above ground in between the raids, otherwise Malta might have been another Pantelleria, and we ran down into the shelters like rabbits if the bombers were too near. I've done it myself.

H. I suppose anything very important like a confinement, for instance, went on down below?

S. Yes, and to succeed in booking a rock chamber for a confinement was no easy task: the wife of one of our Linotype operators wanted one; he said it was vital, for he had married the most nervous woman in Malta! There were the lighter moments, of course, when an old grandfather decided to stay above ground. He was frying fish, difficult to obtain owing to defence coastal regulations at night, and German machine-gunning of fishing boats by day, two-thirds of them were sunk—and he was determined not to let the cat have it, so he made a quick decision and it went against the cat.

H. The worst period of the bombing I suppose was from the end of 1941 to the spring of 1942?

S. That was the third heavy attack. And it was total war. All the farmlands that adjoined gun-sites and aerodromes were filled with great craters; the bombs were ploughing up the food supply,—not that Malta at its best could maintain itself for more than eighty days with two thousand two hundred people to the square mile. We all realised—and I hope you do too—that the men on the guns were heroes—there was never an instance when either a Maltese gun-crew or a crew from the United Kingdom didn't stand by their guns. In March, or was it April, 1942 the gunners fired for 373 hours, equivalent to fifteen days and nights.

H. I remember that during the blitz here, just the sound of our own guns gave us a feeling of security.

S. Everybody feels that in raids. But you see with us, just after the time I've been telling you about, ammunition began to get short and when there was only intermittent fire a certain anxiety gripped the civilian mind.

H. I'm not surprised. How was the air defence at that time?

S. The air defence? The very gallant air defence of Malta had been reduced again to not more than seven planes, so you can imagine the condition of the Island's aerodromes. But those planes flew and it was our infantry—

H. British infantry?

S. Infantry from the United Kingdom and Maltese soldiers who mended the craters and fought for the aerodromes and serviced the planes and unloaded the ships along with Maltese workmen. Infantry filled in the craters for months on end, often surrounded by unexploded bombs, subject to continual attack—and it's no fun just shovelling earth into craters in the target area. As a soldier once said to me, "They may have a war in England, but it can't be just like ours."

H. And you publishing your newspapers all this time?

S. We published seven days a week, and by the way tremendous credit goes to the newsboys—it would have been useless to have printed if we hadn't been able to distribute.

H. Well, you'd scarcely be short of news.

S. We had the front line at the front door and on the front page in the *Times of Malta* and the *Sunday Times of Malta* and *Il Berqa*—that's our Maltese paper.

H. Were your printing machines underground?

S. No, that wasn't possible, but they were sited round a deep shelter my father had prepared—it was a large bell-shaped well which he got ready after the Abyssinian crisis.

H. What I want to know is what food conditions were like in Malta in 1942?

S. I'll tell you. It was June 1942 when the siege settled down on Malta good and proper, grim and cruel. Just beforehand on the 10th May, Spitfires, flown into battle direct from aircraft-carriers, had shot the *Luftwaffe* out of the sky—together with the guns the score was sixty-five in one afternoon, and the *Luftwaffe* pulled out. So the German wireless explained to its public that as Malta was made of rock and was a very tough proposition, "other means must be found to reduce it." "There are 300,000 British who are our prisoners there," they said, "and their Navy will never reach them." That's what they said, and repeated it at intervals for fun. We didn't need them to tell us the seriousness of our position.

H. Lord Gort had taken over the command then, hadn't he?

S. Yes, and he's a great leader. He had made it very clear that both garrison and people would have to be on siege rations, and from May to November the Island faced up to an ever-tightening siege. The phrase 'target date' was introduced, too.

H. What does the 'target date' mean?

S. Oh! I remember being asked that very question in the street and I said "Surely you know enough English to grasp that—it is when the bread runs out"—along with the ammunition and the fuel. And with the realisation that this was actually the test—how long we could make everything last—the Island settled down to preserve all that it could. Plainly Malta had to live on its own resources, and it was fortunate it was summer and the harvest was coming in; but it was a harvest from a land that was as bombed and hungry as the people; there had been no manure or artificial fertilisers since Italy declared war. And there had been no imported cattle to slaughter for meat either. Gort made farmers, conservative like all farmers, realise that unless they shared and didn't hoard neither they nor their Island would survive. The wheat available came straight from the fields into the mills. But before this had happened the time had arrived for the killing of the rabbits and poultry and seven out of every ten Maltese goats. When the killing first started the animals were fit; but then some couldn't be fed at all and an animal loses weight quicker than a human being, so that even a fortnight later there was nothing but skin and bone when they were slaughtered. We suffered heavily because the ship that would bring seed potatoes from Northern Ireland and Scotland failed to arrive.

H. Malta was an exporter of potatoes before the war, wasn't she?

S. Certainly, but the seed, as the farmers knew, had to come from a cooler climate.

H. And it didn't come, so Malta's greatest source of food in peacetime wasn't there?

S. Exactly. The tomato crop that came in August was a godsend, easing up the position for a matter of fifteen days; they were marvellous, and they've got vitamins too.

H. You said August—August was the month when the convoy got through, wasn't it? That must have made things better?

S. I'm glad you asked that. In August, once again, the Navy made the most gigantic effort to get back and to bring supplies to its home. I know that not a man in the Navy could stand the thought of Malta starving. Admittedly a supply had been trickling through with bomber and submarine and the gallant cruiser *Welshman*, but it was a drop, however welcome, in an ocean. The bomber came from too far away to carry much more than its own petrol; and it was no good getting to Malta with little fuel to get back. Five merchant ships of the immortal August convoy fought their way through. They brought flour and ammunition and fuel; aviation spirit, paraffin to cook with, and diesel oil. We had to have that for the pumps which pumped the water from the deep wells underground where it collected.

H. The convoy kept the Island in the fight, but five ships could not in any way alleviate the conditions under which the garrison and people lived?

S. You are right.

H. And what about light?

S. We were months without electric light and gas.

H. And what about cooking?

S. The Government ran a communal meal cooked on paraffin or the wood from bombed buildings, for which 204,000 of the population registered, practically everyone not in the armed forces. The main object of this communal meal being that no-one should starve, or in other words that everyone should starve equally.

H. For if one person was fully fed it meant that someone else had nothing. What did the meal consist of?

S. Oh, one meal: a plate of vegetable soup, one ounce of tinned fish or corned beef, and at a period of comparative plenty what was known as 'veal loaf'.

H. What was that?

S. Slaughtered goats and horses. There was no question of sitting down to the meal, you queued up and carried it away in your own utensils. You could have it either at midday or in the evening.

H. Not both?

S. Not both. I had mine at midday. Besides the meal we got meagre rations of one tin of corned beef a fortnight, a small tin of fish a fortnight, a few beans, coffee mixed with barley and some tea and sugar (sometimes there was no tea and sugar on the ration). Occasionally there were issues of powdered milk, and dried eggs. Tinned milk was only for small children and the sick. There was ten and a half ounces of bread—a third of man's usual consumption.

H. No points?

S. There was nothing to spend points on.

H. In fact there was almost nothing at all. As editor you must have been deluged with letters from the public with complaints and suggestions for the easement of the impossible?

S. Yes; we used to publish a selection of them, too.

H. In other words, you went through all the stages of wartime life we know about here—shelters, bombing, food rationing—with just this difference, that being a small island there was no reserve on which to make any leeway.

S. Rations were very meagre, and whereas the time had been that a bombed-out family could get food from its neighbours and relations, we got to the point where nearly everybody's reserves had all gone—and then the Government bread rations were locked up by the mother of the family.

H. What were the effects of hunger and other shortages? There were shortages of all kinds of things I suppose, as well as food?

S. Well, lassitude, and frayed tempers, and dirt and scabies; and the babies and weak and old die. And everything takes twice or three times the time to do; I used to wonder how the clock would get from three o'clock to six and still material was not ready for the press. And standards went down—our bombed office was swarming with fleas; there was no broom or soap or hot water for cleaning, but who cared except the machine-man who was at his wit's end to keep the machine clean. It was only when life came back that the extent of the human deterioration began to horrify those who had lived through it. While the hunger lasted, small things assumed enormous proportions. Likes and dislikes were unaccountable and continuous, staff would come in and someone would glare at someone and I would say, "Chaps you are hungry and that's all there is to it." The public still wrote letters to the Editor—we filed them because they were history. If it came to the final end, some said, they would shoot their wives and children. All were prepared to go hungrier yet, it was the will of the country. They would never give in to be fascist slaves.

H. What was the worst horror of all?

S. Well perhaps for those who had children. The extent of the siege is thrown into sharp relief if you know that the children would cry at night and an older one would say, "There's no sense in saying 'Our Father, give us this day our daily bread'! It doesn't come." It was in February that my foreman told me, "Miss, I was mad in November, with the children crying." And the faith of the people was tested to breaking point and some blasphemed and most wrestled in silent prayer that deliverance would not long be delayed. I remember one farmer asking me early in November, "How long will it be before the ships come in?" "Oh," I said, "It may be Christmas," and the look of intense pain that crossed his face let me know that there was a breaking point in the growing agony of the battle of endurance.

H. And were the soldiers really hungry too?

S. Yes, the troops were on half rations, and 'Sleep Parades' were held.

H. Sleep Parades?

S. Yes SLEEP Parades—that is they were told to lie down and sleep—so that they conserve their energy and not do anything that would make them hungrier.

H. Many relatives in Britain must have wondered why their menfolk said nothing?

S. Yes, it was information of value to the enemy. However we got to printing the stark word in the paper and there was relief in the fact that for stealing a tin of corned beef worth 2/3d the minimum sentence was two years' imprisonment. The same applied to any food offence.

H. Enforcement of the law was vital.

S. Yes, and it was drastically enforced. Everyone lost weight from two to three stone and Malta became like one vast convalescent home in which everyone existed but was slipping backwards until the siege was raised. Everyone lived in hope of good news from the outside world.

Could such a beleaguered island survive? And yet survive it did.

Churchill kept a constant watch on Malta. "Malta cried aloud for help. The strain was at many points more than could be borne. General Dobbie was distressed. In March he had said that his situation was critical, and on April 20th he reported: 'It has now gone beyond that point, and it is obvious that the very worst may happen if we cannot replenish our vital needs, especially flour and ammunition, and that very soon . . . It is a question of survival.' A few days later he added that bread consumption was being cut by a quarter and supplies would now last only until mid-June." Bread is the staple diet of the Maltese worker, as it was of his Egyptian and Phoenician predecessors, and today connoisseurs reckon Maltese bread as being the best there is. This deprivation, therefore, struck at the very sinews of resistance. The Victory Kitchens were organised to ensure that such supplies as there were should be equally distributed. Cattle, goats, horses, all had been slaughtered for food.

In April, records Churchill, disturbing news arrived about General Dobbie, that 'Cromwellian figure'. At first Churchill was loath to credit it, but he soon became aware that the gallant Governor was worn out and that a new one must be found. Where, in such dire emergency, could be found a man with the experience, the nerve, the courage to serve as the 'daring pilot in extremity'? There was but one. The man who had salvaged an army at Dunkirk and was now leading the embattled garrison on the Rock of Gibraltar, he it was who should be the saviour of Malta. Thus it was that on the 4th May Lord Gort became Governor of Malta. Only one month and seventeen days later, English arms were to suffer a blow even worse than that endured at Dunkirk. After but one day's assault, Tobruk surrendered to Rommel.

Churchill was in Washington at the time. Roosevelt handed him the fatal telegram without a word. Churchill was stunned. Disaster was one thing; disgrace another. Ever since February, Churchill had been urging Auchinleck, who had succeeded Wavell as Commander-in-Chief in Africa, to launch a major attack, so as to regain the airfields of Cyrenaica which were so vital to the defence of Malta. In March he had sent out Sir Stafford Cripps and Lieutenant-General Nye to find out whether Auchinleck's reluctance to undertake an offensive was justified. They were constrained to tell the Prime Minister that it was: to attack piecemeal and prematurely was to invite a defeat which would leave Egypt wide open to the Axis. Nothing daunted, Churchill telegraphed to Auchinleck on the 10th May: "We are determined that Malta shall not be allowed to fall without a battle being fought by your whole army for its retention. The starving out of this fortress would involve the surrender of over 30,000 men, Army and Air Force together with several hundred guns. Its possession would give the enemy a clear and sure bridge to Africa, with all the consequences flowing from that."

Both Churchill and Auchinleck were right: it was Rommel who

The underground granaries at Floriana used for storage of supplies. Soldiers act as porters. St Publius' church was wrecked by bombing.

The Santa Marija Convoy brings deliverance. The *Ohio* limps in between her escorts, and Maltese citizens greet one of the surviving merchantmen.

made the mistake which saved Malta. Auchinleck had finally and reluctantly agreed to attempt an offensive in mid-June: Churchill ordered him to advance it by one month. Auchinleck had no alternative to complying with this order except resignation. But Rommel struck first. The German high command had at last agreed that the 'C3' plan should be carried out. The Italian official history contains nostalgic photographs of landing-exercises by the Italian troops and vessels destined for the attempt. Kesselring had been won over. As soon as Tobruk had been taken, the attack on Malta was to be set in motion.

Tobruk was a tremendous personal triumph for Rommel. He was promoted Field-Marshal the next day. Besides the garrison, he had captured 1,400 tons of petrol, large stores of ammunition, both British and German, 2,000 serviceable vehicles and 5,000 tons of provisions. "It seemed", comments Macintyre, "that all his problems of supply had been solved at one blow." The shame of Tobruk has never been explained. That not everyone agreed with Churchill was well known; indeed, the determination to hold the fortress had been vehemently asserted, and in these matters it is a golden rule to believe nothing until it is officially denied. Perhaps some of this defeatism had seeped down into the garrison. We cannot know. But what we do know is that Rommel's triumph was his undoing. He had always been regarded as a 'short term optimist'. He was now, in the words of the Official Italian History, in a state of "intoxicated enthusiasm" . . . "The glittering mirage of the Delta beckoned him."

Ignoring the Italian Supreme Command, who were his official superiors, he telegraphed to the German Supreme Command: "The morale and condition of his troops, the quantity of stores captured and the present weakness of the enemy make it possible for us to thrust onwards into the heart of Egypt. Therefore request that the Duce be prevailed upon to remove the present restrictions on movement [i.e. the condition that Tobruk was to be a prelude to Malta and no more] and that all troops now under my command be placed at my disposal to continue the offensive." Mussolini agreed. 'C3' was shelved once again—and finally.

In February 1941, Rommel had warned Berlin: "Without Malta,

the Axis will end by losing control of North Africa." That is precisely what it did, and it was due to Rommel that it did so. Malta had still much agony to endure; but it was Rommel who, at its most critical hour, had saved Malta.

12

THE LAST ROUND

1942

'C3' had been shelved—but almost scornfully. Why worry about Malta, when Cairo was theirs for the taking, and in any case Malta was doomed? For although the physical assault on the Island was no longer deemed necessary, the other measures agreed upon at Garmisch, reinforced by later consultations, had been put into operation with deadly effect. The Island was now entirely surrounded by minefields, and mine-sweeping rendered impossible by the unremitting attacks of the *Luftwaffe* on the few available mine-sweepers. Moreover the Island was starving to death.

Clearly, the end was at hand. All arrangements were accordingly made for the Triumphal Entry. The Duce flew to Cyrenaica, and set up his headquarters at Derna, a pretty little town in Eastern Cyrenaica, which had already secured its place in history as the scene of the victory of the American Marines over the Barbary Pirates in the early years of the nineteenth century—the very first appearance of American arms outside the New World. A white steed was procured, and a handsome sword (tactlessly modelled on a Crusader pattern) was ordered for the new Alexander to brandish as he entered the Egyptian capital.

It was at this juncture that I was once more—and never with so much solace—reminded of a remarkable conversation I had had almost three years before with Princess Victoria, the Dowager Lady Milford Haven, and mother of Lord Louis Mountbatten. I had been a guest at Adsdean, the country home of Lord and Lady Louis not far from Portsmouth. Early on the Monday morning, Lord Louis had left for Scotland to visit a new destroyer which was being built there. Lady Louis also had gone on one of the many missions of public duty which she undertook with such ability and charm. I was to be motored back to London later in the morning. Princess Victoria, I supposed, was upstairs in her own apartments. The house was still. I strolled along towards the library and opened the door. There to my utter surprise was Lady Milford Haven, sitting near the window, regally upright and smoking a cigarette. Considerably embarrassed at having behaved in so apparently offhand a manner, I started to back out. "No Mr Perowne . . . come in . . . I want to speak to you. Sit down." And then, "Mr Perowne, there is going to be a war. We know that now. I have seen it all before: we shall see it all again. But remember this, Mr Perowne—they will win campaigns, many campaigns; but they cannot win a war." It was as though the Sybil had spoken, and I have never forgotten the scene nor the sentence. In giving me permission to quote it, Lord Mountbatten recently wrote "I think it only fair to add that my mother must have said 'They cannot win a war against England'. This was because of her conviction that sea power would ultimately crush them and not because she failed to appreciate their victory in the Franco-Prussian war."

This is precisely what happened. Rommel reached the confines of Egypt only to make two unpleasant discoveries. First, although at Tobruk he had captured 30,000 British troops with perhaps a fifth of that number of his own, together with the vast booty already mentioned, he found himself confronted with a resolute and unshakeable army, whose strength in manpower and material was being daily augmented. Secondly, his own supplies were dwindling with dangerous speed. For one thing, Malta which had seemed to be 'neutralised'—at the end of May even its famous 'U' class submarines which had so ravaged the Axis supply lines had been withdrawn—was again menacing the Sicily-Africa run by air and sea. Raeder still pressed for an assault on the Island. Japanese experts, even, were called in to help work out details. But on the 15th June Hitler said to Raeder: "I well know how important the capture of Malta is. All the same, I don't think it can be put into effect while the offensive is being developed on the Eastern front, and above all not with Italian troops . . . With Tobruk taken, the majority of the convoys will be routed to Tobruk, via Crete. Once Malta is held under continuous air attack and total blockade, we might risk the attack."

The Italian Official History sums up the position as follows: "But before all else, besides the opinions of Hitler, and the hesitations of Mussolini, besides Rommel's enthusiasms, the misgivings of the German high command and so many other factors inimical to 'C3', there existed one obstacle of the gravest sort, one detrimental question, which threatened to render useless the preparations which were already in an advanced state and such as to make it feasible to put the plan in operation by the end of July: the oil situation. The naval battle in mid-June [that is, the encounter which had inflicted such heavy losses on the June convoy] had exhausted the last reserves of fuel, so that the Italian warships were no longer in a condition to leave their ports: four battleships had their tanks completely empty: the units which had returned from the action had been unable to refuel, because the tanks, whether in Italy or Tripoli, were also empty."

On the 25th June, only four days after the fall of Tobruk, a conference was held at Derna. Kesselring—who must have been as daring at the conference table as he was in the skies—was adamant. It was useless to talk about advancing into Egypt: it simply could not be done. "At the heart of the problem there always remained Malta."

"In the course of the conference", continues the history, "Kesselring appears to have uttered words which were, alas! only too true: he claimed that the enemy, by withdrawing, had improved his position, while the forces of the Axis had allowed themselves to be dragged a long distance from their bases, without the means of advancing the bases themselves; that at the most it would have been possible to advance as far as Alamein but no farther—'For such a judgment I feel myself responsible before history'—; that finally the enemy's air-superiority would turn out to be crushing; and he concluded: 'I must absolutely mistrust an advance to the end. If the order comes to me, I shall obey it, but I do not know what, in that case, must be the epilogue to the campaign'." But nothing, it was agreed, could stop Rommel now. The very next day, when Kesselring, together with the Italian and German ranking Staff Officers met Rommel at Sidi Barrani, Rommel's enthusiasm, if it did not infect the others, easily got the better of their hesitations. "The troops," said the victorious condottiere of the desert, "are suffering from lack of water and of petrol; but we cannot stop for that. What remains behind will follow as soon as it is in a position to do so: what is ahead fights . . . Our objective is the narrows of Alamein: our ultimate objective the Nile, either to eliminate Alexandria, or finally to advance on Cairo."

The Italian Chief of Staff gave in, and told Mussolini that he could come to Libya. Rommel reached Alamein with reduced and exhausted forces, there to make contact with the far superior English troops arrayed for the defence of the Delta. Throughout July, skirmishes continued with varying fortunes. Mussolini, after waiting for long, and in vain, went back to Italy. Kesselring had been right. Once again, sea power had prevailed. The *coup de grace* would be given by Alexander's famous and victorious campaign. Much has been made of this, and, in the right hands, rightly. But it is well to remember that the knell of the Axis in North Africa was sounded in the summer of 1942, and that it was Malta that tolled its doom. To Malta we must now return.

'C3' had been tacitly abandoned; but starvation, which has terminated so many a siege, threatened the Island more than ever.

At the height of that awful summer, it was decided to take the risk of sending two bombers by night to Cairo, carrying some of the worst afflicted mothers and children, Maltese and English. Those who received the sufferers were appalled by what they saw: women hardly able to stand from the ulcers on their legs and bodies, children so wasted by undernourishment that the slightest abrasion of their starved limbs might endanger their lives, so thin had their blood become.

Submarines, a swift minelayer, might bring to the Island much needed stores; but they could not possibly supply the Island with the means of survival. Lord Gort took immediate and practical steps to ensure that such supplies as might reach Malta should be preserved. At long last, the Grand Harbour was girdled with smoke canisters. The effectiveness of these canisters may be deduced from the following note by Mr Oreste Vella, a Customs and Excise Officer in the Port Department, at the Custom House, Marina, Valetta, who was a Boarding Officer. "As such," he writes, "I had to board ships on arrival from overseas, and these included those that arrived in the convoys of 1941 and 1942. We were then fighting for our own personal existence coupled with the daily frequent alarms of attacks from the air, and the shortage of our daily requirements of food-stuffs and ammunition for our survival. This gave me little time to keep records of my day to day experiences; in fact I do not have any special recollections. We simply had to attend to the ships in a hurry, as frequent air-raid alarms sounded, and if we had time we were compelled to leave the ship to seek shelter ashore; but many a time we had to remain on board when smoke screens were used and I could not find the way to shore. This was an awkward situation as ships in harbour were the constant target for the German planes."

Unloading was speeded up. Troops were called in to assist stevedores. Every lorry in the Island was commandeered, and each was painted with a colour which indicated its destination. Similarly coloured signposts were placed at essential points on the routes. A Maltese policeman accompanied every vehicle to prevent looting. Despite the sparse stocks of fuel remaining, Lord Gort decided to hold a dress-rehearsal of this exercise, and it was well that he did. The circumstances are best explained in an official notice which was published on the day after the first rehearsal:

"The Public will have noticed a number of lights which were placed at intervals along certain roads on Saturday night. These lights were placed there in connection with an important military operation, the successful outcome of which is essential to the defence of Malta. The exercise will be repeated on the night of Monday, 15th June.

"On Saturday night many of the lights were removed by members of the Public, either because they feared the glow of them would be visible from the air or because they wished to use the lamps in air raid shelters.

"Tests have proved that these lights are NOT visible from the air.

"It is essential that the lights are not removed or extinguished or the lamps borrowed or stolen. Anyone touching any of the lights in question will be 'Helping the Enemy' by lowering the efficiency of the garrison of the Island. The Police have accordingly been instructed to take severe action against anyone found touching, extinguishing or pilfering any of these lights."

At the last moment, the streets and roads were cleared of any but essential traffic, so that all stores should reach their destination as rapidly as possible.

But where were the stores?

The fate of the June convoys has already been related. During July, the Germans, Kesselring included, were right in declaring once again: "*Malta ist sturmreif*": Malta is ripe for attack.

The attack never came. Throughout July and during the early days of August, supplies continued to arrive in Malta, carried in submarines and in the very speedy mine-layer *Welshman*, each consignment prolonging for a few days the possibility of resistance. Nevertheless, supplies were now lower than they had been in April, so low in fact that Lord Gort and his expert advisers had to face the fact that unless the Island was replenished, there was only one course open to them—surrender. Evacuation was impossible. As always the Government took the people of Malta into their confidence: they spoke to them, over the rediffusion network, with complete frankness. Already, on the 16th June, Lord Gort explained the failure of the two convoys which were intended to bring succour to the Island. Four days later, the Lieutenant-Governor, Sir Edward Jackson, enlarged on the topic. "If the enemy failed in his main purpose, he succeeded in part of it. He has delayed the arrival of our much needed supplies, and as His, Excellency the Governor has told you, a time of further privation, greater privation than we have known hitherto, lies ahead of us . . . We received about 15,000 tons of stores from the two ships which arrived. That is something and certainly a help, but it is a very small part of what we had hoped for." After giving a full analysis of the stocks in hand, and mentioning the rather curious fact that despite everything the Malta bread ration, which it was intended to maintain, was just over the normal Italian one, Sir Edward uttered the following ominous words:

"I have said that in examining our position, we first calculated the time for which our bread could be made to last. That calculation gave us a certain date which I shall call the 'Target Date' the date to aim at. Our next task was to see how we could make our other vital necessities last to the Target Date." This was simply a tactful way of saying that if supplies did not arrive in fairly good time, the Island must surrender or starve to death.

And so the historic 'Santa Marija Convoy' as it has come to be known was mounted. Churchill himself took a leading part in its organisation.

This famous operation, which was to save Malta, had a curious prelude, which Mr E. S. Tonna has fortunately preserved for us. On the 5th August, Lord Gort paid an official visit to Floriana. "On arrival His Excellency was met by Mr S. Galea (formerly Commissioner of Police and now retired and) District Commissioner for Valetta and Floriana, who presented each committee member to the Governor . . . During Lord Gort's visit to Floriana, Mr S. Galea pulled me aside and told me that he came to know from very reliable sources that Malta would be completely out of the war by October 1942. I could not possibly believe my ears considering how the Island was besieged and how difficult it was for essential supplies to reach Malta. On pressing for more definite news Mr Galea's exact words were: 'When October comes I shall give you more definite news.' And when October came the Battle of Alamein started which routed Rommel and his Afrika Korps. Was it this which Mr Galea wanted to convey?

"I was suspicious at the time that Mr S. Galea had obtained this information from Lord Gort himself and this could have been the case because Lord Gort was told about the possibilities of the Middle East offensive campaign and the North-West Africa landings by Field Marshal The Viscount Alanbrooke when the latter visited Malta on the 2nd August, 1942, on his way to Egypt.

"It is recorded in Alanbrooke's War Diaries *The Turn of the Tide* that he wanted Lord Gort to know about this to make him feel 'that if all this came off he would find himself in an outpost of an advance instead of backwater he considered himself in. I feel certain that to be able to look forward to something definite would do much to dispel his gloom'."

The following quotation from *The Turn of the Tide* supports Mr Tonna's thesis.

"For the next hop it was essential to reach Malta before dawn, otherwise there were chances of being shot down by Italian fighters. Dill and Eden on their way to Greece had missed the Island, overshot it and had to turn back to find it, only reaching it just in time. I was specially anxious to visit Gort in Malta as I knew he was in a depressed state, feeling that he had been shoved away in a corner out of the real war and in danger of his whole garrison being scuppered without much chance of giving an account of themselves. His depression had been increased by the fact that he insisted on living on the reduced standard of rations prevailing in the Island in spite of the fact that he was doing twice as much physical and mental work as any other member of the garrison. Owing to the shortage of petrol he was using a bicycle in the sweltering heat, and frequently had to carry his bicycle over demolished houses.

"*I wanted to tell him about the plans for the new Command in the Middle East with an advance westward, combined with American-British landing in North-West Africa moving eastward, destined to meet eventually. I wanted to make him feel that if all this came off he would find himself in an outpost of an advance instead of the backwater he considered himself in. I felt certain that to be able to look forward to something definite would do much to dispel his gloom.*"*

* A distinguished contemporary of Lord Gort told me recently that he thinks that Alanbrooke's estimate of Gort's mental state was justified. Gort had become a national hero for his conduct of the evacuation of Dunkirk; but that at the time when he was sent to France he had been in the running for another appointment which he did not receive. Even his achievements in Gibraltar and Malta may not have effaced his feeling that he had been *limogé*.

The same authority told me that he thinks it possible that Lord Wavell, famous for his exploits with Allenby in the first war, and for his defeat of the Italians in the first winter of the second, never realised the difference between defeating a Turkish or Italian army and overcoming a German one.

"Had Brooke known the secrets of the German General Staff he would have had even more to tell his old chief about the Island's part in the overall strategy of the war. For that spring it had been agreed by Hitler and Mussolini that Malta was to be invaded from Sicily by four airborne divisions, two of them German, with a sea-borne expedition guarded by the Italian fleet as soon as the bridge-head had been secured. This operation had been planned for July, but after the capture of Tobruk, Hitler postponed it till September on the ground that it would involve needless loss if, as then seemed probable, Rommel could capture Egypt and the Canal without it. (Shulman, *Defeat in the West*, pp. 59–60.) The fight put up by the British in Crete a year earlier was still vivid in his memory and he shrank from the risks and sacrifices of another operation over the sea. Like most Germans, his strategic outlook was continental and, despite the entreaties of his admirals, he failed to grasp the close connexion between Malta and the battle Rommel was preparing to wage for the Nile Delta. It was because Churchill and the British Chiefs of Staff were so well aware of it that at that moment the Admiralty was preparing to send a major fleet into the western Mediterranean to fight a convoy through to Valetta at all costs."

These paragraphs from Arthur Bryant are paramount in explaining just what the visit of the C.I.G.S. meant to Malta, and how very significant was the conversation, reported above, between Salvo Galea and Lolly Tonna.

Alanbrooke's own impressions of that fateful 2nd August are recorded in his diary.

"After lunch went down to the docks and to Valetta. The destruction is inconceivable and reminds me of Ypres, Arras, Lens at their worst during the last war. We travelled about in the Admiral's barge and examined wrecks of the last convoy. Finally examined new dock workshops which have been mined in the rock. Had tea with the admiral in charge of docks. Five air-raid alarms during the day, but no serious bombing. Finally at 10.45 p.m. just as we were about to start, a German plane came over but did not remain.

"It had been a hot and tiring day, all the more so after a hard day in Gib. and two nights' flying without much sleep, sitting up with a wooden box between my legs. The visit had been well worth while, and I think brought a new hope to Gort. The conditions prevailing in Malta at that time were distinctly depressing, to put it mildly. Shortage of rations, shortage of petrol, a hungry population that rubbed their tummies looking at Gort as he went by, destruction and ruin of docks, loss of convoys just as they approached the Island, and the continual possibility of an attack . . . without much hope of reinforcements."

Such was the background to the colloquy between Salvo Galea and Lolly Tonna on that historic day. As shown, in particular, by the sentences which I have placed in italics, Alanbrooke fully understood the vital rôle which Malta had played in defence and was now to assume in victory.

Clearly some great and salutary event was in the offing. On the 4th August Churchill was in Cairo. I happened to be there, too, for an official conference. One afternoon, as I was passing the Embassy, I saw a number of solemn people converging on the entrance. Their bowed heads and heavy looks led me to think that someone had died and that a memorial service was about to be held. But when I joined the throng, whispers soon made me realise how wrong I was. We assembled in the ballroom, and then, from the left hand side there shuffled onto the dais the well-known figure, clad in his battle-dress and wearing his monogrammed velvet slippers. He was greeted with rapture. I suppose he spoke to us for a few minutes only before, after giving his victory sign, he went his way on more important business. But how he had transformed us. We strode out into the city with heads held high, proudly conscious that we belonged to a victorious nation.

Five days later, General Alexander was in Cairo, about to assume command of the Desert Armies. One evening, when I got back to my hotel, I was told that Lady Killearn wanted to speak to me. On the telephone, she asked me to come to dinner that evening. On arrival at the Embassy, I found myself a member of a very small company, namely the Ambassador and Lady Killearn, General Alexander and his aide-de-camp and myself. Throughout dinner, and afterwards in the garden by the Nile, I sat entranced, enthralled by General Alexander's conversation. He talked quietly, slowly, as he told the tale of the war in the far east. It was a doleful story, a story of defeat, of error. But not once did General Alexander utter one word of extenuation. He simply gave us the facts. "He might be an observer from another planet," I said to myself, "he talks as Thucydides wrote." By the time I took my leave, I was firmly convinced that such a general must lead our armies to victory, and it was to overwhelming victory that he led them.

It was at that very time that the most famous convoy in history was entering the Mediterranean, for the salvation of Malta. 'Operation Pedestal', as it was officially known. It was, as already emphasised, essential that it should reach the Island. Plans for surrender had in fact already been drawn up. These were naturally kept within the knowledge of a very few people. But here, as always Lord Gort showed himself a wonderfully acute psychologist. The Maltese are an intensely devout people—a novena of prayer was at that very time being held. The priests were always at hand to comfort and support their flocks. They would carry the sacred Mysteries through bomb-shattered ruins. In the dankest shelters the Rosary was regularly recited before the weary inmates sought such rest as they might. Among the most respected pastors in all Malta is Monsignor Salomone, 'Dun Edgar' as he is universally known, parish priest of Mgiarr, where his enthusiasm has caused to be erected one of the finest churches in the Island. Dun Edgar had been an Army chaplain during the first war. He was the personal friend of Admiral Fisher and of Sir Harry Luke, both of whose names are commemorated in the streets of Mgiarr. Not long ago, I recalled a conversation I had had a few years ago with him, and, together with Sir Harry, went to call on Dun Edgar, who is now over eighty. "Dun Edgar", I said, "what was it that Lord Gort said to you?" The old warrior looked puzzled. Prompted by Sir Harry, I said, "About the surrender." At once Dun Edgar sprang into action. "It was there," he said, pointing to a chair. "There he sat. He said he had come to tell me something serious. 'If the convoy does not arrive within four days, we must give up. I have it here'," and the old priest at this point slapped the pocket of his old soutane three times, " 'the document of surrender'."

It was as near as that.

The story of the Santa Marija Convoy has often been told, never better than in *Malta Convoy* by Peter Shankland and Anthony Hunter. That the enemy had intelligence of the convoy, of its destination and of its importance is beyond question, as anyone who has read *Malta Besieged*, by R. Leslie Oliver, who was in Malta at the time, must be aware. Admiral Syfret in the *Nelson*, with the *Rodney*, three large carriers, seven cruisers, and no less than thirty-two destroyers, entered the Mediterranean on the 9th August for Operation Pedestal. This armada escorted fourteen fast merchant ships, one of which was a brand-new tanker, the *Ohio*, a beautiful ship lent by the United States, whose navy had requisitioned her from the Texas Oil Company. She was one of the fastest and finest vessels of her kind. She was specially prepared for her great mission. Two A.A. guns, a 5-inch and a 3-inch were fitted. Her engines were placed on specially designed rubber housings, because the breaking of a pipe by a near-miss bomb had made it necessary to sink a former American tanker, the *Kentucky* which had sailed in the ill-fated June convoy. The *Ohio* loaded a full cargo of 103,576 barrels of petrol at Sinclair Terminal, Houston, Texas, and set out for the Clyde. Here she discharged her cargo, and her master and crew were told that they were to hand over the ship to the British. Clearly some special mission was in view. Her armament was considerably strengthened and her ship's company of seventy-seven had been selected from among the most experienced and reliable men available, with Captain Mason in command. The *Ohio*, whom its British crew insisted on calling the 'OH-ten', was loaded with 11,000 tons of kerosene and diesel oil fuels. The other ships bore a grand total of 85,000 tons of cargo. The bulk of supplies loaded was flour, but each ship carried some petrol and aviation spirit in tins, together with some other explosives.

The experiences of the convoy are summarised by Churchill. On the 11th August, the Admiral's fleet was off Algiers, whence its presence and composition were at once reported to the enemy. The carrier *Eagle* was the first victim, sunk by a U-boat. The *Furious* successfully flew off her Spitfires to Malta, whence they were to provide vital air cover. The next day the expected air attacks began. One merchantman and a destroyer were sunk, and the carrier *Indomitable* damaged. Thirty-nine Italian aircraft and an Italian submarine were destroyed.

The most dangerous part of the journey was now about to begin. The convoy was approaching 'The Narrows', that is the channel between Cape Bon and Sicily. This channel is about 100 miles wide, and experience had painfully proved that large, capital ships could not be safely manœuvred there, owing to lack of sea-room, and the presence of the fortified Italian island of Pantelleria almost equidistant from either shore. This meant, that any convoy bound for Malta must, for the last 170 miles of its journey 'run the gauntlet', attacked by Italian aircraft, U-boats and E-boats, and protected only by its own lighter vessels and Malta-based aircraft. On approaching The Narrows, therefore, on the evening of the 12th, Admiral Syfret with the battleships withdrew according to plan, leaving Rear-Admiral Burrough to continue with the convoy.

The night that followed brought a crescendo of attacks by U-boats and E-boats, and by morning seven merchant ships had been lost, as well as the cruisers *Manchester* and *Cairo*. Three other merchant ships and two cruisers were damaged. Damaged, too, was the *Ohio*. Undaunted the survivors held on for Malta. Daylight on the 13th brought a renewal of the air attacks. Besides another merchantman, the *Ohio* was hit again. This time she was stopped, and became simply a 'sitting duck'. By skilful management however, she was got under way again. After the second hit she was taken in tow by the destroyer *Penn*; but the huge rent made by the torpedo in her side made towing impracticable. The ship was abandoned. Later, she was again boarded, and again, as by some miracle got under way. Once again she was hit, once again abandoned, once again taken in tow. She was being continually attacked and was steadily sinking. But at last she sighted Malta. Her steadfast captain and her remarkable rescuers had devised a novel and wholly unconventional method of keeping her afloat. Instead of attempting to tow her, they held her up, one on either side of her. And thus it was that she reached Malta at last. No ship had ever made so wonderful a voyage, survived so many hazards, brought to land a more vital cargo. For his share in this exploit Captain Mason was awarded the George Cross.

The *Ohio* entered the Grand Harbour on Sunday, the 16th August. On the preceding day, the *Port Chalmers*, the *Melbourne Star* and the *Rochester Castle* arrived safely. They were joined later by the crippled *Brisbane Star*. The losses, both of warships, and of aircraft and of merchant ships, had been appalling. But Malta was saved.

Mr H. F. White, who as Chief Steward of the *Rochester Castle* was mentioned in despatches for the part he played during the Santa Marija Convoy, wrote an account of it from which he has very kindly allowed me to quote.

"Whilst in New York after, or rather during, the most eventful voyage of my twenty-three years at sea, a voyage I am at present still completing, I met aboard his ship my old Chief Steward Mr L. C. Clauson, a man whose opinions and adaptable cleverness I have long respected; I was aboard his vessel on a combined business and pleasure visit, the business side of the meeting was to try to arrange for the transfer of some linen and other items which the ship I was on, being then about ten months without having renewed her stock, was badly in need of.

"Mr Clauson had heard stories of my ship's (I cannot give name of vessels) eventful voyage, and was very interested in snatches of our adventures which I related to him, and suggested that while the trip was still fresh in my mind I should put it in writing 'It will be interesting later on,' he said, well it may be—to my wife.

"Now I wish to make it clear that this is my own version of what happened and whilst it is as true an account as I can make it, it may not be accurate regarding times and would certainly not agree with many another man's view aboard my own ship, and again I have tried to forget some of the more horrible sensations . . .

"The ship sailed from Liverpool on a nice sunny afternoon,

Sunday, 21st June . . . The following evening our ship docked at Glasgow, and within a few hours the crew had the 'genuine' information as to our destination, when the rumour reached me I knew it to be true; for I had spoken to Sea Transport Officers 'in the know' and was aware we were bound for Malta with badly needed ammunition and food; one 'cheerful fellow' told me he did not envy us, as the last convoy to go to that place had been badly mauled only two ships out of six arriving, and then they were sunk in harbour—I found this to be true later . . .

"On Friday 10th July we left Glasgow fully loaded for Gourock where the convoy was made up. Most days I was ashore for some reason or other—the ship was at anchor—and always managed to get a trunk call through to my wife, who to my knowledge had no idea as to the nature of the trip I was about to make, and yet she may have, for she remarked on the large number of guns the ship was armed with; I tried to pass it off with 'It's the usual thing now'. Much of our time at Gourock was taken up with 'gun drill', boat drill, fire drill, sometimes at night, and viewing films to help in the identification of aircraft, all of which was inconvenient and annoying at the time, but later to prove invaluable to us.

"By this time [Saturday 1st August] the whole ship's company was well acquainted with what to do 'in action' from the captain to the lowest rating everyone had been drilled to his particular job, by virtue of my rank I automatically became 'in charge 1st Aid Party', but as I had no qualifications for this I relegated myself to second place in favour of the Medical Orderly. In this party was a steward from S. Ireland who when asked to take a course in gunnery jokingly replied 'I'm neutral', whether that was his true reason for not manning a gun I don't know, but he lacked nothing in the way of courage when the ordeal came.

"8 p.m. Sunday 2nd August our anchor was hauled up, and our adventure had commenced.

"Outside the boom-defence—what a peculiar sensation that always is, crossing the safety line—we were joined by our R.N. escort, some destroyers, corvettes and a couple of light cruisers; we had fair weather for the next week, and had it not been for the manner in which our escort of R.N. ships was increased it would have been an uneventful voyage, but we were now nearing the Straits of Gibraltar, and we were a really formidable fleet; fleet is the right word; two 1st line battleships H.M.S. *Nelson* & *Rodney* (with 16 in. guns) a number (I guess eight) cruisers including the latest types, five aircraft carriers and a screen of destroyers stretching from horizon to horizon in a semi-circle ahead of the convoy of fourteen swift merchantmen, we were the slowest vessel, 18–19 knots, and the only single-screw ship amongst them. I heard German reports on the wireless later that it took eighty-five warships to get this convoy through—that may be true.

"For the benefit of the superstitious, our ship's number in the convoy was *13*, and our position 1:3—first line, third ship, which placed us at the tail end of the line, not an enviable position, but the whole convoy was constantly changing position, four lines, three lines, etc., and I shall never forget Lieut. Binham's calls to the 'bunting tossers',' Answering Pennant' and 'Down Signal' as the orders to manœuvre were sent from the battleships to us, and from my observation the exercises seemed to be carried out satisfactory, but were a headache to our navigating officers; they all seemed to be 'on watch' all the time.

"Our speed and course had been so directed as to enable the convoy to pass through the narrow entrance to the Mediterranean Sea under cover of darkness, this we did, and it was faithfully broadcasted by the neutral Spanish Radio the next morning.

"Depth charges were now being dropped in greater frequency by the destroyers, we had been accustomed to the ship jumping and quivering as they exploded under sea for some days now, we did not know whether they denoted the proximity of submarines or whether they were dropped as a precautionary measure.

"By Tuesday, 11th August we were well in 'Mussolini's Ocean' and until 1–15 p.m. everything going fine, I was in such good spirits that I wrote in a letter to my wife—it was never posted—'I wish you could be here to see this wonderful sight'; the convoy, it was that day we received a signal from the Commander-in-Chief, Admiral Syfret telling us of the hazards of the days ahead, and advising everyone to sleep or rest as much as possible, the message ended 'We must not fail the people of Malta.'

"Three tremendous explosions and a 'different shake' at about quarter past one caused me to go on deck to investigate; I heard someone call 'the *Eagle*'s been hit' and sure enough when I saw the aircraft-carrier she was already listing, and planes falling off her flight deck, destroyers were dashing towards her, dropping depth charges as they went, we 'carried on'—the convoy *must* get through, and soon she was just a blur on the horizon, astern, our first casualty; I am sure the 'sub' which torpedoed her let us pass for 'better game' as the *Eagle* was in line astern of us, the tail end ship of the convoy at that time.

"We knew we needed aircraft-carriers and the planes they carried so you can imagine the loss of one had a subduing effect on us; but things began to happen soon after that which did not give us time to mourn. Previously we had been warned 'No more practice stations, in future all signals (on bells etc) denote the real thing.'

"Up to this period I have been able to keep pretty near times and days, but from now on I lose all sense of time and confuse days. Well every minute threatened to be my last, so why should I have bothered about time? that was my reaction to my first experience of *heavy* action.

"The ringing of 'three A's' on a shrill bell near my cabin on that Tuesday afternoon, denoting 'aircraft attack' made me grab my 'tin hat' which I had up to then regarded as an unsightly ornament— we wore life-jackets permanently—and dash to the mess room which was the casualty ward, but as we had as yet no casualties I decided to see what all the firing was about. Our ship was firing from the after Bofor, so I went that way, the gun's team were holding their fire for a few seconds, but had the gun trained on a 'plane circling the stern of the convoy, remember we were the 'tail end'.

"Lance Bombardier Clough R.A. was in charge of the Bofor at the time and when he gave orders to resume fire I watched our shells (and tracers) explode perilously close to the plane, until after a few rounds during which time the plane had passed our stern and was coming up on the port side he scored a direct hit on the tail of the plane and it dived into the sea about a mile off our port beam. We could hear the cheers from other ships, and our ship's company yelled! I found myself 'clapping hands' and thinking 'Take that for the *Eagle*' then I thought of the pilot of that plane, whose husband or son was he? out there with no hope of rescue, the convoy carried on—it *must* get through.

"This affair seemed to me to be 'a good seat at the pictures', surely *I* could not actually be mixed up in an action like this—it was only a few days ago I was at peaceful Gourock in Scotland.

"I did not see this plane drop any bombs and assume it was a reconnaisance flight, and the pilot was able to radio our position back to his base before being hit, for at dusk we were attacked by a considerable force of German planes, and what a barrage those R.N. ships put up! The din was terrific, how long this action lasted I cannot say, but 'Jerry' was still trying in the darkness and the different coloured shells shooting into the heavens was a sight never to be forgotten.

"I don't think we had any supper that night, we were so 'worked up' or busy, nobody went to bed, for we were constantly at 'stations' and we knew there were some 'subs' about; before daybreak the dive-bombers were at us again, and kept the attack up, coming in from all directions, but the dangerous ones came 'out of the sun' and were hard to spot, but the Fleet Air Arm was up too early too, and fought off a large number of squadrons out of our sight. The Fleet Air Arm claimed ninety-seven planes shot down during the whole battle.

"It was inevitable that some of the merchantmen and escorts should be hit by such heavy and long attacks as this, and about 11 o'clock (a.m.) the ship in line ahead of us caught a bomb on her after-deck, and appeared to be sinking with a list to starboard, we passed quite close to her, and I saw her crew clearing away the life-boats, they called or cheered us as we slid by, and it hurt me to see that as close as we were we made no attempt at rescue, 'The convoy carries on, it *must* get through.'

"Again those hardy ships were there, destroyers rushed up to the damaged vessel, but we were too far away for me to see what happened, but imagine everyone's surprise when later this same ship came up with us! but alas, she soon stopped an aerial torpedo and sank.

"Attacks by aircraft continued the whole day, there may have been an occasional break of half an hour when there was no firing and during one of the spells I managed to get some eggs hard boiled and distributed to the men at stations in gun pits and on the bridge or anywhere around the decks, coffee and tea I had managed to keep going all the time, and the men just helped themselves when they could, the Irishman and I were the only ones in the Stewards' dept. not allocated to a gun.

"During some of these attacks one ship seemed to be the objective of all planes and the (famous) *Ohio* a tanker came in for her share of this treatment, then as plane after plane tore down on her in a 400 mile an hour dive, every gun in the convoy H.M. ships and M.N. would throw a screen of shells over and around her, or any other ship which was attacked in this manner, we had our share, I remember on one occasion when I had a message saying a man had been hit on the after gun. I had collected what equipment I thought I should need including a basin of water and with 'Paddy' who never seemed to leave me was going aft to attend to the man when 'Paddy' yelled, 'Look out boss, duck', away went the water, and I was laid out on the deck just as a 'big one' swished into the sea, just feet away, a few splinters came aboard and scratched paintwork and an avalanche of water, from where I lay I watched six more Stukas dive down AT US and release their bombs, two fell near where the first had fallen starboard quarter and four on our port bow, none of them could be measured as yards away, and nobody could call that 'luck' we had no atheists aboard then. Was I scared? sure I was, and mad, too for I kept thinking of my wife at work in her office in Southampton, and *laughed* to think what she would say if only she knew at that moment what I was doing.

"We had news about midday this day (Wednesday) that the Italian fleet had put to sea to intercept us, and I think this caused a more wide dispersal of the convoy, leaving the *Rodney* and *Nelson* in the centre of it, we saw their huge guns being trained, and waited for the enemy to show up, but of course these two ships could have sunk the whole Italian fleet out of sight. Around 4 o'clock we had another shock! fourteen enemy torpedo carrying planes (one for each merchantmen?) came tearing in at us 'out of the sun' about 200 feet above sea level, they got close in then, boom! and the 16-inch guns of our two battleships opened up: when the smoke cleared only one plane was visible, ahead of the convoy and soon he was on fire and crashed into the sea, the concussion and blast from those mighty guns had 'capsized' the other thirteen . . .

"By Wednesday evening the convoy was approaching the most dangerous part of its voyage to Malta, the narrow strip of water about seventy miles wide between the N. African coast and Sicily, which is dotted with small but useful Italian owned islands, which they have turned into submarine and E-boat bases, the most powerful is Pantelleria; knowing these narrow channels had been heavily mined by the enemy our paravanes had been swung into position earlier, thus slightly reducing our speed . . .

"This night the big battleships left us, their part of the business accomplished, to fight their way back again, which they did.

"Just after 3 o'clock on the morning of Thursday *13*th August our ship received her biggest 'bump'. I was off my bed with the sound of the explosion, and grabbed the 3rd's leg as he struggled to get off the settee. I said to him 'Stay there, while I go and see what has happened–I'll be back.' He said, 'I'll tell you: that's her lot, a torpedo.'

"Looking out from the Officers' Entrance (starboard side) I could just distinguish in the darkness number one lifeboat (mine) hanging useless by the forward fall, and the ship was taking a list to starboard and forward, sea water everywhere; running back to the cabin I said 'I'm afraid you're right, come on what's your boat number? No 1 is gone'. . .

"From the time we were hit naturally I moved fast, and what I have described [collecting stores and so forth] did not take much time, so that when I arrived back on the boat deck again the crews of the lifeboats were sorting themselves out, everybody was standing back in favour of somebody else–I would not believe it if I had not seen it–I was in a hurry to get in a boat, but me the first?

"All this time we were being shelled by an E-boat, and now he seemed to have our range proper, for 'pings' and 'whirrs' were sounding all around us. The skipper yelled 'Take cover or let the – – – – –have one–Man the guns, we can hold for a while.' Back went the crowd to action stations and Sgt Pearson, who had not left his forward Bofor gun, got in an awkward angle shot, and up went the E-boat which (he claimed) had torpedoed us . . .

"Somehow we seemed to draw away from the dive-bomber and E-boats for we enjoyed a quiet spell for an hour or so and that gave us an opportunity to try out the pumps on No 3 hold, where we had been hit; it was a 'toss-up', sometimes the pumps won, then the water, but there did not appear to be any immediate danger of our sinking, and dawn found us afloat and alone; later a 'smudge' on the horizon coming up astern of us was clearly a warship of some kind, we thought at first an Italian, but she turned out to be one of our light cruiser escort, and soon we picked up about four more merchantmen and some destroyers, and to our disgust some more German aircraft, for they soon found us again in those narrow waters, and they were well aware of our destination; the attacks and evading action of the previous day started all over again, the dive-bombers coming in in waves at short intervals.

"After such a night as I had had I did not feel too fresh, bathing was out of the question, but I decided a shave would help a lot so I tried it, and had just finished when in comes another wave of 'Stukas'; I still had my life-jacket on, so all I had to do was to get my 'tin hat' from my cabin; whilst doing so I heard the plane diving down, then the bombs whistle as they were released, I guessed they were intended for us, and not wishing to be caught inside made a dash for the deck, this was madness really and useless because of the nature of our cargo; I heard the bombs shriek overhead as I gained the entrance and thought 'The blast will blow me back inside', so I put my back to the bulkhead and intended to brace my arms out on the opposite one, as I did so, I noticed my hands were shaking so badly they were turning a quarter circle, this made me laugh and I steadied up a bit, then, a tremendous explosion and the highest and most terrific sheet of flame, triangular in shape, and topped with black, shot up from aft of us. I thought 'My God, her stern has gone' amd waited (unconsciously) for my feet to get the 'vibration' from such a hit, not feeling it I was just about to step out onto the deck when I heard another 'whirr' and stopped, something thudded onto the deck I did not stop to see what, but running to the ship's side, and looking astern I saw 'the sight' which (nearly) demoralised the remainder of the convoy—ours was the only vessel NOT to issue rum as a stimulant—about 200 yards astern of us I saw the bows of the '— — — —' only about ten feet of them vertical and rapidly disappearing beneath the water. I was so shocked and moved (that does not convey my real sensations) that I could not stop and watch her 'go down'; I had a 'vision' of the *inside* of that ship, can YOU get it? those men, no chance, the engineers below, a man in his cabin where his deck head in *two seconds* becomes his bulkhead and in two more his cabin becomes his tomb.

"The R. Navy was there again, and although this sank *instantly* they saved *thirteen* men; later I spoke to some of the survivors—stewards—one told me he 'jumped' and while in the water beside his ship heard things falling inside her and the 'swish' of the engines as they tore away from their bed and raced the ship to the bottom of the sea.

"Things looked pretty grim for us now, as the size of the convoy and escort had sadly diminished, three merchantmen, one cruiser and a few destroyers; we were again 'tail end' now that the 'W— — —' had gone, and from the way the aerial attacks were being launched it was obviously our turn next, I, and I have reason to believe every man aboard this ship, prayed as we had never so sincerely prayed before; I had visions of my home; it was sunny and peaceful there, but what when *that* telegram arrived? morbid but natural thoughts I suppose, for our position seemed hopeless to me, badly holed and slowly sinking, travelling at a reduced speed and God knows how many miles to go, a hot sun and no sleep, we did not have much appetite for what little food was to hand, and surely 'Jerry's' crack 'yellow-nosed' airmen could not go on so narrowly missing us! one very near miss had 'started' the plates in the engine room, but the pumps were able to handle that as well as our 'big hole', another 'close one' astern had sent two fragments directly at our 4.7 gun, one piece penetrating the barrel, and the other piece down the muzzle spoiling the rifling, so that the gun was useless . . .

"Never has one day been so long; reassuring messages kept coming from the bridge 'Stick it, we shall be there in seven hours, six hours' and so on; but events of the day were crammed in each hour.

"I issued beer to the men, starting while it was 'quiet', but I think 'Jerry' thought he was on the list too—for he came. I did not try taking money, but wrote down the men's names as they took a bottle, but the list was useless, the first occasion I could not read my own writing.

"During that morning I was laid flat out 'inside my tin hat' on deck with a junior engineer who WAS a hero, he was almost as scared as I, and when it was time for him to go below on watch, he said he could not go down using many persuasive arguments and giving him a drink of sal volatile I eventually managed to make him reasonable and he went on watch.

"This young man has not been at sea long and experienced the big Blitz on London; with us he had done his watch in the engine room and manned a gun during his 'leisure hours' ever since the attacks started.

"I think our last aerial attack was about midday on this day Thursday *13*th August, but it was much like all the previous attacks had been and not worth describing, of course we did not know then it was to have been our final one and when it was over, we busied ourselves getting ready for the next one, clearing gun pits of empty shell cases, getting fresh rockets in position, and clearing the debris from its unaccustomed places around the decks where it had been placed by 'near misses' and heavy rolling of the ship as she took quick turns in evading action.

"When I had done my share I laid down on the deck to rest. I must have fallen into a 'doze' for I awoke with a start to what I thought was the sharp 'crack' of Oerlikon guns, but it was 'Chippy' nailing canvas on a large hole on the side of No 3 lifeboat; it was later discovered that *all* our lifeboats were badly holed and not one service-

able; so it was fortunate we did not abandon ship earlier that morning.

"Some time that afternoon the alarum for action stations rang again, planes approaching on the starboard bow, then quickly the order came, 'Hold your fire, believed friendly.' My God! I didn't think there was such a thing as a friendly plane.

"The formation of planes drew closer, then circled the convoy (or what was left of it), signals flashed, but we already knew them for 'Spitfires'. I believe the ship herself sighed; and we cheered! This was what we wanted aerial protection, what a relief.

"Shortly after, the cry of 'Land in sight' sent us all crazy with delight, the rocky shores of Malta were near.

"Looking up at the bridge I saw the captain looking 'spick and span' in his white uniform. I know he had not left the bridge since passing Gibraltar, so I took the hint, had a good bath and change and also donned 'whites', feeling much better I went on the bridge and seeing the Captain said 'Thank God we are here, sir.' He replied, 'We are *not* yet, this is the worst few yards, heavily mined by enemy aircraft last night.'

"Malta was well in sight now, and looking ahead I saw two minesweepers and some torpedo boats approaching, they swept a passage for us, and flashing a 'Thank you and good luck' signal to our only light cruiser escort, which—after all this—was going back to Gibraltar, we limped into Valetta Harbour about 6 o'clock, slightly down at the head, boats hanging useless in the falls, a hole eighteen feet by twenty in No 3 hold, plates leaking in the engine room, and machine-gun bullet and shrapnel holes everywhere, our paravane when hoisted aboard looked like a jelly fish where undersea explosions had battered and twisted it . . .

"As each ship entered fresh cheers rolled out, and continued until we had all berthed; as this ship was in a sinking condition we were 'laid on the mud' and a pontoon of lighters connected us with the shore; doctors and medical orderlies boarded us immediately and Mr Seaward and Lockhead were hastily examined then rushed ashore to hospital; this was an event for more cheers and handclapping, some of the women were crying, and all had sympathetic words for our injured. 'Jerry' had not finished with us yet, for before we were properly berthed the air-raid signal sounded ashore, but 'Spitfires' went up and kept them away from the harbour.

"Arrangements to land our valuable cargo had been made previous to our arrival and this work was put in hand immediately; these ships were not going to be sunk [before being] *unloaded* as the two previous ones had been . . .

"Around 8 o'clock a naval launch came alongside and took us ashore to sleep under the rock of Malta. As I was climbing down a rope ladder to get into this launch I heard the air-raid signal sound again, and wondered if the ship would still be afloat in the morning."

Ironically enough, Malta's saviours, for such they were, did not realise to what extremity Malta had been reduced; they did not understand that those who had cheered them as they entered the Grand Harbour were at their last gasp, or that their smiles masked starvation. Naturally, the one longing of those who had made that awful voyage was to enjoy 'the blessings of the land'. They went ashore as soon as they could. Two seamen were walking in the dark of Floriana that evening, when they encountered a citizen. Where, they asked him, could they find a nice restaurant or café? The officer—for such he was—looked at them blankly: did they not know, he said, that there had been no restaurants nor cafés open in Malta for many a long day? Seeing how crestfallen they were, the officer then invited them to be his guests, and so they found themselves shortly afterwards in a family shelter, cut in the rock, where the family were about to eat a very frugal evening meal. This they willingly shared with their English guests. On taking their departure, the sailors begged their host to lend them a pillow-case, and to meet them the next evening, by the ruined portico of St Publius' church. At the hour appointed, the Maltese officer reached the ruined church. Out of the gloom appeared his friends of the night before, with the pillow-case. This they handed over, and at once disappeared, leaving the pillow-case with their Maltese friend. Inside it, there was a gammon of bacon.

Early the next morning, one of the ships' officers, who had enjoyed a quiet and restful night ashore in a naval dugout, was taking a stroll, when he came on an anti-aircraft post. The men were brewing tea. He walked over to them and asked whether they could give him a cup. "Well," was the reply, "there's only just enough to go round once; but since you are an officer from the convoy, we'll put some more water in."

. . .

The Axis commanders were dispirited. A German admiral, Churchill says, "recorded: 'a more useless waste of fighting power cannot be imagined. The British operation, in spite of all the losses, was not a defeat, but a strategical failure of the first order by the Axis, the repercussions of which will one day be felt'." The Italian history is sourly succinct. "In this same month of August, in which the abandonment of 'C3' was finally sanctioned, there arrived in Malta, in the course of Operation Pedestal, five out of fourteen vessels, besides the usual *Welshman*, despite the keen opposition of the air and naval forces of the Axis. It was the first substantial replenishment to have reached the Island for a year: not enough to allow of an increase in the meagre food rations, but in any case of sufficient importance to ensure some further months of resistance. That was due to happen in October, because the siege was running to its end.

"From the tenth to the twentieth of this month there developed the final aerial offensive against Malta, for which Cavallero had asked during the whole of September. On the 5th he had written: 'I have been insisting on this point for a long time. If Malta is neutralised we shall win all the battles in North Africa, if it is not we shall lose the lot.' Kesselring had replied that his forces were inadequate, his pilots worn out. 'The men had developed a state of nerves which he defines as "Malta fever".' Again on the 30th September, he wrote 'Importance of Malta—whoever says "the Mediterranean", Egypt included, says Malta.' The results of the assault were undoubtedly scanty. Then, too the great battle of Alamein was beginning and after the 20th October practically all the surviving German air force in Sicily were thrown into the Egyptian inferno. When, one month later, the great convoy *Stoneage* arrived without loss in

Valetta, the Maltese were able to reckon that for them, at last, the war was over.

"And for the Axis it was irremediably lost: the English had arrived at Agedabia, and were marching on Tripoli: the Americans had disembarked in North Africa to deliver from there the first attack against the European fortress; the German Sixth Army was surrounded at Stalingrad, and the Russians were advancing on the whole of the now exterminated Eastern front. From that time onwards, the projected assault on Malta was no more than a memory. On the 20th October, the very same day on which the Germans relinquished for the last time the attack on Malta, Mussolini confessed to Cavallero: 'You know, all things considered I have come to the conclusion that instead of advancing on Mersa Matruh, it would have been better to carry out the operation against Malta'."

To return once again to Malta. The ships of the Santa Marija Convoy were speedily and safely unloaded. By a remarkable engineering feat, the oil was pumped out of the *Ohio*, while sea water was pumped in to keep her from breaking her back, until, with the last drop of her vital cargo salvaged, she sank gently to the sea bed. She had found rest at last. The arrival of the convoy had been greeted with delirious joy, with cheering crowds, with a band playing 'Rule Britannia' on the harbour mole. There was, quite naturally, disappointment that rations could not immediately be increased —that must wait until October. But let Mr Tonna tell his own story, for it is the story of Malta told by a Maltese patriot.

"It was mid-August 1942. The imposing, mellow bastions, built by the Knights of St John overlooking the Grand Harbour of Malta were seething with crowds watching what was left of the Santa Marija Convoy to Malta moored in the still blue waters of this mid-Mediterranean sentinel . . . Malta had already been subjected for months on end to very intensive bombing and the enemy was determined to neutralise the Fortress. . . . Enemy ships on their way to Tripoli and Tunis were being continuously harassed by bombers from the Malta airfields and hence it was vital that the garrison be deprived of reinforcements and the populace made to starve and revolt.

"But the Axis powers were underestimating the fibre the Maltese were made of and which was equalled by the sheer determination of the British Naval Authorities to raise the siege of Malta at all costs.

"On the 15th August every year the Maltese celebrate the Festa of Santa Marija commemorating the Ascension of the Blessed Virgin Mary, Mother of God, into Heaven. In peacetime this Festa is celebrated with great pomp and solemnity as there are seven parishes in Malta and one in the nearby Island of Gozo dedicated to Santa Marija.

"In 1942—the peak year of aerial bombardment over Malta—there were no outdoor festivities on the 15th August. The people were not in a mood to celebrate; they looked haggard, depressed and desolate over the fate of their country. War damage was visible everywhere, most of the buildings in the Grand Harbour area had been razed to the ground and life in general had been relegated to the underground rock shelters. This is where the majority of the Islanders used to pray, cook their scanty meals and sleep on deck chairs and stools, always hoping for a silver lining to appear across the blue skies of Malta.

"A few of the convoy ships including the tanker *Ohio* very badly battered by enemy bombers in the Sicilian channel struggled into the Harbour on the eve of Santa Marija Day, and the Maltese, with tears in their eyes, cheered the brave ships from the tops of the bastions and the quaysides. They crossed themselves in thanksgiving to the Queen of Heaven and earth, as it was, as they believed, through her intercession that replenishments had reached the Island and thus the blockade would be lifted. This is known up to the present day as the Santa Marija Convoy Miracle. Malta was to keep alive and free."

The technical and strategic outcome of this momentous year, in so far as it concerned Malta, was succinctly put in a broadcast, recorded in Malta itself, on the 14th January, 1943, by the Air Officer Commanding, Air Vice-Marshal (now Air Chief-Marshal) Sir K. R. Park.

"A most interesting feature of 1942 has been the way in which the besieged island of Malta passed from a purely defensive to an all-out offensive rôle between July and November 1942. During the winter of 1941, Malta was being attacked steadily by enemy bombing forces based in Sicily and the Royal Air Force was mainly employed in the close defence of the Island. A small amount of bombing, however, was carried out against enemy ports and shipping. Also, the Royal Navy Air Squadron carried out a number of successful torpedo attacks against enemy convoys. In the Spring of 1942, Goering and Mussolini evidently decided to neutralise Malta to prevent the squadron attacking the Axis convoys running from Europe to North Africa. A greatly superior enemy air force was concentrated in Sicily and carried out intensive and sustained bombing attacks by day and by night and practically overwhelmed the modest fighter defence in March and April 1942.

"For nearly a month in fact the Island and our aerodromes had to rely almost entirely on the A.A. batteries of Malta which put up a magnificent defence. In spite of this intense and almost unrestricted bombing, the ground staff of the Royal Air Force carried out essential work on aerodromes and when the Axis withdrew their bomber forces from Sicily in May and the blitz ended, the Royal Air Force recommenced attacks on enemy shipping.

"The attacks on shipping by the Royal Air Force and the Royal Navy Air Squadron caused the enemy in July to launch a further, though less intense, bombing offensive against Malta. This time the bombing attacks concentrated entirely against the Royal Air Force Aerodromes, but after a couple of weeks' hard fighting, our Spitfire squadron obtained complete mastery of the air over Malta. Our fighter squadrons then carried the offensive into the enemy in Sicily, and we redoubled our attacks with torpedos and bombs against enemy shipping proceeding to North Africa.

"These convoys were badly needed by Rommel in Egypt and we sought out and attacked many hundreds of miles from Malta both by day and by night. In the autumn of 1942, in October to be precise, Goering and Mussolini decided that it really was high time to put the Royal Air Force, Malta, out of action once and for all. Goering concentrated in Sicily a bigger bomber and fighter force than ever before, and on the 11th October launched a second blitz against Malta. Although greatly outnumbered our Spitfire squadrons went out half a dozen times a day to meet the oncoming enemy raids north of Malta and gave the enemy such a sound thrashing that the blitz ended after ten days of hard fighting. During this October blitz, the Axis endeavoured to run a large number of important convoys from Europe to Africa. In spite of the almost continuous daylight bombing, the Royal Air Force Squadrons made a record number of attacks against enemy shipping . . .

"In November 1942 the Anglo-American expedition landed in Algeria and the Royal Air Force based on Malta launched a new offensive in support of this adventure . . . General Eisenhower commanding the Anglo-American expedition in Africa, sent the Royal Air Force, Malta, a special message of thanks for their great support given to his expedition during November and December. Shortly after the Anglo-American expedition had landed in Algeria, General Montgomery began his attack on the Germans in Egypt. The squadrons based on Malta again helped the 8th army by attacking the enemy convoys by day and by night and so preventing supplies reaching Rommel."

. . .

What the arrival of the convoy meant is perhaps best shown by an article in the weekly *Information Service Bulletin*, dated 21st August, 1942 and headed "A promise kept–What Malta's convoy means."

"Our feeling of tension is at an end. The ships have arrived and so far, strangely enough, the enemy has made no attempt to interfere with our unloading them. We have been relieved but the siege of Malta has not yet been 'raised'. That may not happen until the Victory of the United Nations–and even after Victory it will inevitably be some time before the supply situation in Malta can be restored to normal.

"Perhaps the most encouraging feature about the convoy for us in Malta is that a promise has been kept. Lord Gort V.C. said last June that 'Every effort will be made to replenish our stocks, and the successful effort that has been made to do so has been breath-taking in its courage and determination.' Sir Edward Jackson said in June 'England will not forget us and her Navy and Air Force will see us through.' His words have come true and will come true again . . .

"The naval operation to bring us supplies was on a par with the desperate exploits of Elizabethan mariners, it was in the tradition of Drake and the *Revenge* . . .

"By sending us this convoy the people of Britain have shown us that the strength of their solidarity with us far transcends expressions of admiration and the conferring of decorations on us for the part we have already played; beyond that they are prepared to sacrifice ships, and sailors' and soldiers' lives not only to keep us in being as a fighting force, but to save us, their brother British citizens from the worst privations of siege conditions, than which the only worse fate is that of the Greeks and our other allies who have fallen into the maw of the Axis beast . . . Most of us have met some of the splendid men who have survived this battle and we have heard at first hand tales of bravery and horror which have amazed us. War is hell—as we have learnt—and their experience was hell at its worst—fire and water, the hair-raising terror of Stukas screaming down at one's own particular ship, seeing the bombs come out of the plane's belly and curving down towards one, the nerve-shattering uproar of a stick of bombs bursting close round in the water, and then feeling the huge ship leap under one like a spurred horse. And all the time they stuck to their guns—and down below were the engine-room staff with hardly a dog's chance if their ship were badly hit. That was how the promise to us was kept. A pledge that has been redeemed with our fellow-citizens' blood.

"And even so this sacrifice has not relieved us of all our troubles. What those troubles have been and will continue to be—is freely acknowledged by the men of the convoy themselves. 'We know you are the bravest people in the world,' said a convoy captain to the writer of this article, who also overheard a sailor say, as he gazed round Valetta, 'This place has certainly been bashed.' The chief feeling of these gallant men was one of satisfaction that they had done their job and brought us the supplies we so badly needed.

Another of them said that after he had seen and talked with the people of Malta he would be prepared to go through the ordeal again if called on to volunteer to help us."

The article ends with a call for still greater austerity and discipline on the part of the inhabitants.

That is the instant and actual effect of the arrival of the Santa Marija Convoy. Even after twenty-five years it has an immediacy which no later account can convey.

NOTE: The *Welshman* (pp. 140 and 172) was a racing mine-layer, one of a class of four. She was of only 3,100 tons, but was equipped with engines of 75,000 h.p. (half the power of the *Queen Mary*). She could therefore make forty knots. She carried many vital cargoes to Malta, such as ammunition, seed potatoes and tinned milk. She was Churchill's pet, and at the conclusion of each successful mission (her executive officer Lieutenant-Commander Ian Cox, D.S.C., tells me) he would make her a signal: "Well done." With her sister mine-layer *Abdiel* she accounted for forty enemy vessels. She was sunk off Tobruk on the 1st February, 1943, about half her ship's company being rescued.

EPILOGUE

"Hear now the conclusion of the whole matter."

By 1943, the battle was won, the siege was over. Thus does Alanbrooke sum up the situation:

"On the day on which the Prime Minister and Brooke left Washington [26th May, 1943] after 600 miles of channel had been swept by the Royal Navy, the first British convoy to pass through the Mediterranean since 1941 reached Alexandria without loss. The attempt of the Italians and Germans to make that sea an Axis lake and break across the Nile Valley into Asia, so nearly successful, had cost them nearly a million casualties, 8,000 aircraft, 6,000 guns, 2,500 tanks, 70,000 trucks, and 2,400,000 tons of shipping. Its defeat was as momentous as Stalingrad and achieved at far lower cost. From Alamein and the first 'Torch' landings in November [on the 8th November, on the Algiers beaches] to the final surrender in May, the Allies had lost little more than two per cent of the ships they had sent into the Mediterranean and only 70,000 men including wounded. By its re-opening they reduced the length of the passage from Britain to the Middle East from 13,000 to 3,000 miles—a saving of forty-five days on the average time of every convoy—and gained the equivalent of at least a million tons of shipping."

Yes, Malta was saved, saved by sea power and by the resolution and devotion of its people and garrison. And, on the testimony of friend and foe alike, Malta had played a major part in the irrevocable defeat of the Axis, and the restoration of freedom to Europe.

To return to Miss Strickland's interview:

S. By the 26th November the first four ships had made Malta unmolested.

H. What happens when a siege is raised? What do people feel like?

S. Well, there was thirteen days of siege ration food left when those four ships came in. It's a funny thing, but people were much more patient when the siege was on, than when four ships came in and they thought they could feed 300,000. It was not till Christmas that things eased at all, though ships were coming, pouring in. But, you see, we were still in the front line and they still had to bring food for the guns as well as for the people. We stopped being hungry in March.

H. That didn't mean that there was anything touching luxury?

S. Like jam, for instance, or even oatmeal. Perhaps the most wonderful experience was as the Island came back to life. Just before I left in May I heard of a broody hen sitting on twelve eggs.

H. And that seemed like a miracle?

S. Yes, everything seemed so different. I walked over some farm land in March this year and the farmer said how grateful he was that the sky was filled with the British planes. There was a new type in the sky that morning—an American Lightning. The people called the aeroplanes *tana*, ours. Suddenly the farmer stopped in front of a hole in the ground. I said, "Hallo, what do you do down there?" "That is the shelter," he said, "where I and the English prayed." "Which of the saints did you pray to?" I asked him. He threw his hands to heaven and said "*Kull Hatt*—all of them without distinction."

H. And the fight which the people of Malta put up through nearly two years of siege and air bombardment—when over 1,500 enemy aircraft were shot down over the Island—the fight that Malta made during those terrible months and years saved Egypt as certainly as the battle at el Alamein saved Malta.

S. Yes, Mr Hastings, that's true. Malta has seen great days since then—a visit by the King, the invasion of Sicily . . .

H. From which the main attack on Malta was made.

S. And whose conquest Malta made possible by her own epic fight and the miracle of her survival. And now at last we've seen Fascist Italy fall. And today,* as you said at the beginning of the talk, the Italian battle fleet sailed into Valetta Harbour to surrender.

* 11th September, 1943

This event made the people of Malta deliriously happy and was a great reward for all the suffering of the siege. Malta and its garrison showed the world what they were prepared to endure.

The siege had to be experienced to be realised and you cannot easily imagine either the fortitude or the organisation required to withstand it.

Those dark and glorious days are hardly more than a memory now. A new generation has grown up, to see Malta not only free and happy, but for the first time in her long history a sovereign state. Her hospitable citizens receive visitors from all lands, and none are more welcome than the Germans and Italians. The happy little children who play in their seaside garden at Gzira know not that it is laid out upon the rubble of ruined houses in Valetta and the Three Cities. In Valetta itself, only the ruins of Barry's Opera House remind the wayfarer of the war. The railway tunnel is sealed up and forgotten, the famous 'Yellow Garage' gallery once again houses vehicles, not refugees. Vittoriosa still shows some piteous scars, but only for the older citizens do they hold any sadness. Here and there in the countryside a strand or two of rusty barbed wire, or a few old army oil-barrels, protect a field. Beneath the windows of what was Oliver Ormrod's Mess the immemorial rhythms of seed-time and harvest have returned; and the jolly scarlet lorry that romps round Rabat, called 'Sink the Bismark' (for in Malta all the lorries have names) raises no more than a nostalgic smile. The old hulk of the *Ohio* was towed out to sea on the 19th September, 1946, and sunk by gunfire. On the 3rd November, 1956, H.M.S. *Illustrious* was sold for scrap and broken up at Faslane in Scotland.

Twenty-five years after the arrival of the Santa Marija Convoy Mr White and seventeen other survivors attended a reunion in Malta on 11th August, 1967. "One of the first sights to greet us," Mr White later wrote, "the next morning was a small coaster discharging her cargo under our windows. Her name was *Queen of Peace*. What a contrast to our first morning in Malta twenty-five years ago when we were met with bomb and anti-aircraft fire."

Lord Gort once quoted General Monk's words, uttered in 1671:

"There is as much honour gained by suffering want patiently as by fighting valiantly, and as great achievements effected by one as by the other."

Malta had done both.

MELITA SUPEREST

APPENDIX

Army strength and duties

On the 3rd September, 1939, the garrison of Malta consisted of the following:

The 2nd battalion of the Devonshire Regiment.

The 2nd battalion of the Queen's Own Royal West Kent Regiment.

The 1st battalion of the Dorsetshire Regiment.

The 2nd battalion of the Royal Irish Fusiliers

The 7th A.A. Regiment, Royal Artillery (in 1940 renamed 7th H.A.A.).

The 1st battalion, King's Own Malta Regiment.

By the end of September two more voluntary battalions of the K.O.M.R. were embodied. The Malta Auxiliary Corps had been formed, whose members reinforced existing corps.

In November 1939, the garrison was classed as a Division. A draft of officers and men arrived.

In May 1940, the 8th battalion of the Manchester Regiment arrived; in September 1940, the 27th H.A.A. The addition of eight 3·7 mobile guns and twelve Bofors almost doubled the gunfire density.

In February 1941, the 1st battalion of the Hampshire Regiment, and the 2nd battalion of the Cheshire Regiment arrived from Alexandria. The Buffs were almost up to 1,000.

In February 1941, the Malta Government introduced conscription: national service for all males between sixteen and sixty-five and military service for those between eighteen and forty-one.

The army had to guard ninety miles of coastline. It constructed 300 pens for aircraft. It contrived twenty-seven miles of disposal-area between Hal Far and Luqa airfields, known as the 'Safi strip'. The

R.A.F. had no ground staff. Ta Qali airfield was cared for by the Manchesters, Luqa by the Royal West Kents and the Buffs, Hal Far by the Devons. On some days, 3,000 men were at work. The army transported supplies when landed. They furnished boarding-parties for contraband patrols.

In April 1942, Malta's *airfields* received a weight of bombs twenty-seven times as great as that which had fallen on Coventry in October 1940. In May 1942, sixty-four Spitfires reached the Island. Between the 1st June, 1941 and 13th July, 1942, it is estimated that 693 Axis aircraft were destroyed over Malta by the R.A.F. and ground fire. The last major attempt was made on the Island in October 1942, when it took ninety-eight fighters to escort fourteen bombers. The attack was abandoned after eight days. On the 20th November a convoy from Egypt reached Malta intact. For the invasion of Sicily Malta harboured more than thirty squadrons of aircraft.

SOURCES

A. *Oral.* In a study which treats of the events of twenty-five and more years ago, many of the chief characters are, inevitably, with us no more. I feel the loss particularly keenly in the cases of Mr J. Axisa, a dear friend who was Commissioner of Police during the Siege years, of Sir Edward Jackson and of Sir Andrew Cohen, two brilliant and resolute men who contributed notably to the final deliverance. 'Dun Edgar', alas (p. 157), died in 1969, while this book was in the press.

Fortunately, many survivors have been able and generously willing to help me. I have acknowledged their assistance in the text. But I must here make particular mention of Mr Michael Kissaun, Mr Emmanuel Tonna, Mr Herbert Ganado and Mr John Bezzina, because not only did they give me much valuable information, but put me in the way of obtaining more from others.

B. *Contemporary.* A number of books were written at the time of Malta's ordeal:

The Epic of Malta, Odhams, 1943.

The Unconquered Isle, Ian Hay, Hodder and Stoughton, 1943.

Malta Invicta, Bartimaeus and others, Chatto and Windus, 1942.

Four books are of especial interest:

Le Mie Vicende, by Sir Arturo Mercieca, Casa S. Guiseppe, 1947.

For Gallantry, *Malta's Story by a Naval Wife*, written in 1943 by Mrs Norman, and published in Ilfracombe in 1956.

Malta at Bay (1942) and *Malta Besieged* (1943) by R. Leslie Oliver, a highly skilled journalist who wrote on the spot (Hutchinson).

To these may be added Official Notices, the *Times of Malta*, and diaries, of which by far the most poignant are those of Oliver Ormrod, which Miss Strickland, who had been granted permission to publish them, very generously put at my disposal. Finally, there is Miss Strickland's 1943 broadcast, and the other B.B.C. interviews.

C. *Later Historical Works.*

A Sailor's Odyssey, by Admiral of the Fleet Viscount Cunningham of Hyndhope is a classic foundation book for the whole story. So, in its insistence on the vital importance of Malta, is Churchill's *Second World War. Cunningham of Hyndhope, Admiral of the Fleet* by Oliver Warner is also valuable.

Of works devoted specifically to Malta and the Mediterranean *The Battle for the Mediterranean*, by Donald Macintyre, and *Malta Convoy*, by Peter Shankland and Anthony Hunter are of the highest merit.

The work which tells the whole story from beginning to end, most objectively, and in the greatest detail, citing every available source in Italian, German, French, English and Japanese, is that published in Rome in 1965 by the Ufficio Storico Della Marina Militare, compiled by Mariano Gabriele and entitled *Operazione C3: Malta.*

S.H.P.

INDEX

ITALY
Naples
Bar
SARDINIA
Palermo
Messina
SICILY
The Narrows
Tunis
C BON
Augusta
Syracuse
PANTELLERIA
MALTA
MEDITERRAN
TUNISIA
Tripoli
0
100
200
Miles
0
100
200
Km
L I